clare
a light in the garden

CLARE

a light in the garden

She was the first flower in Francis' garden, and she shone like a radiant star, fragrant as a flower blossoming white and pure in springtime.

St. Bonaventure

Murray Bodo

Quotation on page 50 is from *The Spirit of St. Clare* by
Heribert Roggen, copyright © by Franciscan Herald Press and
used with permission.

Translation of the Letters of St. Clare to Blessed Agnes of
Prague in the appendix is by Father David Temple, O.F.M.

Illustrations by John Quigley, O.F.M.

Cover and book design by John Quigley, O.F.M. and
Julie Van Leeuwen.

SBN 0-912228-54-7

For Mary, the mother of Jesus
and my heavenly mother;
For my own mother whose love
is greater than any I know;
For Sue, whose love made
this story possible;
And for Deborah, who believed
it could be written.

Table of Contents

Sometimes, more often than we think, there are souls so pure, so little earthly, that on their first meeting they enter the most holy place, and once there the thought of any other union would not merely be a descent, but an impossibility. Such was the love of Francis and Clare.

Paul Sabatier

Foreword

The first biographer of St. Clare, Thomas of Celano, began his work in 1255, soon after her canonization, and completed it the following year. *The Legend of St. Clare of Assisi* draws heavily upon the canonical process and document of canonization and the testimony of eye-witnesses to the life and sanctity of Clare. It is a small volume of 44 pages, but it zeroes in on the essential elements of her life.

Since then other books have been written about Clare's life, her spirituality and the nature of her contemplation. This book is not that kind of book. It pretends to be neither a biography nor a spiritual meditation upon Clare's life. Nor is it a portrayal of the life of the Poor Clares. It is a story based upon Clare's relationship with St. Francis of Assisi. Their friendship opened my imagination to a whole new dimension of story.

This is that story as I discovered it visiting the places dear to Clare and Francis, and writing down the thoughts that came to me on my journey. Because the book is largely an account of the part Francis played in Clare's life and she in his, it is a story of intimacy, but an intimacy of mystery and space. Clare and Francis reverenced the mystery in each other and allowed enough space between them to preserve that mystery.

The story is not necessarily always factual, but to me it is true. And if you believe, as I do, that the imagination sometimes brings us closer to truth than does fact, then perhaps you can dare to believe that the imagination can also remember something history has failed to record.

Murray Bodo, O.F.M.
Casa Papa Giovanni
Assisi

Chronology

In comparison to our knowledge of St. Francis, very little is known about St. Clare and even less about the relationship between them. The following is a brief chronology of Clare's life around which I have built this story. This chronology and list of a few available English texts may prove helpful to the reader who is unacquainted with the main events of her life.

1193 or 1194	Birth of Clare of Assisi, descendant of the noble family of DiFavorone.
March 18-19, 1212	Clare leaves home after hearing Francis preach during Lent. She is received by Francis and his brothers at St. Mary of the Angels; beginning of the Second Order of St. Francis.
	Clare lives in a little convent near the church of San Damiano where life consisted of great poverty and strict penance.
1215-1216	Clare becomes abbess; she obtains the Privilege of Poverty from Pope Innocent III.

1218-1219	Cardinal Hugolino becomes "Protector" of the Poor Clares and gives them a strict Rule.
1224-1225	The beginning of Clare's long sickness that lasted until her death.
October 3, 1226	Death of Francis.
September 17, 1228	Pope Gregory IX renews the Privilege of Seraphic Poverty.
1240-1241	Clare, by her prayer, frees her convent and the city of Assisi from the Saracens of Frederick II.
1247	Innocent IV gives the Poor Clares a new Rule.
1248	Cardinal Rainaldo becomes the "Protector" of the Poor Clares.
1252	Cardinal Rainaldo confirms the Rule of Clare.
1253	Pope Innocent IV confirms the Rule of Clare.
August 11, 1253	The death of Clare.
August 12, 1253	Burial of Clare at San Giorgio.
August 15, 1255	Canonization of Clare.
October 3, 1260	Transferral of the body of Clare to the Basilica of St. Clare, Assisi.

Further Reading:

The Legend and Writings of St. Clare of Assisi, The Franciscan Institute, St. Bonaventure, New York, 1953.

Saint Clare of Assisi, by Nesta de Robeck. Milwaukee, Bruce, 1951.

The Spirit of St. Clare, by Heribert Roggen. Chicago, Franciscan Herald Press, 1971.

Francis: Bible of the Poor, by Auspicius Van Corstanje, O.F.M. Chicago, Franciscan Herald Press, 1977.

A Springtime Story

It is good in Assisi in the spring, when the poppies on the plain below the city break wild and red in the air. You walk beneath the clean blue heavens that spread the clouds above the mountains, and you are somewhere between two paradises—one overhead and one at your feet.

It is good in Assisi in the spring because this is the city where a love began, a love not diminished by the years. One man and one woman, Francis and Clare. So great was their love for God that even now, seven and a half centuries later, it makes Assisi good in spring and summer, fall and winter, too.

Their story, this Francis and this Clare, has been told many times; yet like every good story the telling of it is always new, and some further truth may be revealed in telling it again. The Franciscan message is the story itself, and it has something to do with Assisi in the spring becoming summer, surrendering to the gentle mists of fall, lying seemingly dead in winter, and waiting for the poppies of another spring.

The lives of Francis and Clare are themselves seasons of every soul. This book is part of that story, Clare's story, and therefore Francis' story, too. And it is more a story of springtime than any other season of the year. It is a story that looks heavenward but is always rooted in the poppy fields in the plain below Assisi.

Sky and earth and flowers.

The Treasure

She followed him because she loved the treasure. She heard him speak of what he had found, and a passage in her own heart opened up. They had found the same treasure in different caves, and they would share it with whomever they met in that sacred place below the surface of life. She was Clare and he was Francis, and together they would show the world its hidden heart.

Clare was only 11 that day in the Piazza del Comune when she saw this young man gone "mad." He, the rich son of Pietro Bernardone, was making his way across the piazza, unkempt and haggard, begging food from the cursing citizens. Her young eyes were transfixed at this incredible sight, and she did not understand what he was doing. She, with her child's mind, thought he was funny and began to giggle, trying at the same time to wriggle free of her mother's firm grip. She wanted to run after him and join in all the mocking "fun" the grown-ups seemed to be having.

The following year when she was 12, a strange scene was enacted between Francis and his father in the cathedral courtyard. Later she heard her parents talking in low voices about Francis, the wild 24-year-old son of Bernardone, and of how he had renounced his father before Guido, the Bishop of Assisi. She wondered what "renounced" meant and why the bishop was there. But this time she didn't laugh. She sensed in her parents' voices a terrible seriousness. What Francis had done was something evil, something good children never do, and that night her sleep was filled with nightmares of beggars and bishops and fathers red with anger. Francis had already begun to haunt her.

By the time she was 14, he had become something of a celebrity, if still an oddity, a name on the lips of everyone in Assisi. He had repaired the crumbling churches of San Damiano, San Pietro and Our Lady of the Angels with stones he begged in the city. He lived with and nursed the lepers on the plain below Assisi, and he had changed his hermit's garb for that of a barefoot preacher.

And then she heard him preach. The words were simple and unadorned, but they touched her like a deep and purifying shaft of light. Her whole being seemed bathed in a light that came from somewhere inside her own heart.

What it was that Francis had opened up she did not know. It was not merely a fascination with Francis himself that drew her, but his words and something inside the words—the treasure, a secret, powerful force that came, she was sure, from God himself.

Her soul thirsted for more, and she longed to hear Francis whenever he preached to the people. But she was still in her teens and did not have the freedom to come and go as she pleased. She would, however, find a way. She would find a way because what was happening inside her came from God. She saw in Francis someone who must be experiencing what she felt in her own heart.

It frequently happens that a woman attains to greatness in the natural or supernatural order because she has built her life upon the ideals of the man she admires . . . . This is particularly true of St. Clare. It is impossible to think of her apart from Francis.

Lothar Hardick, O.F.M.

A New Love

She was in love! With God? With Francis? With both of them? With love? How did you sort it all out? Or should you? She was to learn over and over again the difference between loving and being in love, but this was the first time, and it was all too much for her.

She threw open the shutters of her bedroom and leaned out in the morning freshness, her gaze resting on the facade of the church of San Rufino, the patron of Assisi. She and Francis had been baptized in that church, and she had made her first communion there. Her father's palazzo was adjacent to the church, so she had grown up, as it were, in the courtyard of the church of San Rufino. And now during this Lent of her 18th year, Francis had been preaching from its pulpit.

What he said inflamed her heart as nothing ever had before, but so did Francis himself. He seemed always to be looking only at her and to be speaking to her alone. At first this had disarmed her as she sat

4

next to her parents in the first pew and looked into his penetrating brown eyes. How small he would look as he mounted the pulpit and how large he would grow with every word that struck her heart.

And then their long talks together, the flame burning bright in her soul. Francis must have known how she felt about him, must have wondered how he was going to handle what was happening inside this young, impressionable girl with the golden hair. Oh, how she missed him just thinking about him this Palm Sunday morning!

The sun had not yet climbed to the top of Mount Subasio, but the light of dawn had preceded it into her little square, and she kept her eyes on San Rufino. Shortly the town would begin to wake with the clatter of shutters, and bells would ring in the sun of another day. And she would go to Palm Sunday services for the last time with her family.

For Francis and Bishop Guido had finally decided that this would be the day of her leaving the world to follow Jesus Christ as a spiritual daughter of Francis Bernardone. She would be the first woman to believe and follow the dream of poverty and littleness that God had given Francis for the rebuilding of his kingdom.

And this very night it would all happen. Clare was so in love that the coming of night seemed an eternity away. These last hours would be the longest of her life, for just below the city in the little chapel of St. Mary of the Angels someone divine and someone human were waiting for her. She was in love, her heart rushing to begin loving.

5

A Consecrated Life

By her vows of poverty, chastity and obedience, Clare was wed forever to her Lord and Savior Jesus Christ. But in that solemn ceremony when Francis himself took her hair into his hands, cut through her curls and watched them fall onto the dirt floor of the chapel something else happened as well: She was wed in mind and heart to Francis.

Even externally she became like him. In a ritual that mirrored Francis' own stripping of himself before the Bishop of Assisi, Clare placed her satin dress into the hands of the brothers and put on a rough woolen habit. She secured it about the waist with an ordinary rope more beautiful to her than the jeweled belt she wore in her father's house. And with naked feet she stepped into a pair of wooden sandals that shone like golden slippers in the candlelight from Mary's tiny altar. Now they were one, she and Francis, alike in everything from the dream they shared to the very clothes they wore.

She would hold fast to the total poverty of this ecstatic moment till the end of her days. Now she and Francis shared everything that mattered to her in life. What greater union could there possibly be than union in the Lord? Clare viewed that moment of consecration in the Portiuncula* as a sacrament of her union with her Lord and with Francis. He was now bound to her and she to him by their common consecration to the Lord. She was as much a part of his life as were his own brothers—perhaps more so because she was a woman and he a man. In some transcendent yet tangible way they were building a new Eden in which men and women walked in the cool of the evening hand in hand with God.

They had both stood naked and innocent before God and man: Francis when he stripped himself in front of the crowd gathered before Bishop Guido

---

*Portiuncula means "little portion" and is the term of endearment Francis used for the little chapel of Our Lady of the Angels.

and she when she placed her lovely dress into the brothers' open palms. Now there was nothing worldly between her and Francis; the Lord was there, and they would walk at either side of him forever.

The Lord stood between them, but he was transparent. They saw each other even more clearly through the radiance of his glorified body. His presence made their union more real to her because it was beyond space and time and yet grounded in the most tangible of all realities, the human heart and mind, the human soul and body. What woman or man could ask for more here where all is not yet perfect, here where evil is still a reality to be reckoned with, here where the cross is still the only chariot to Heaven?

Those who observed Clare and Francis with purely human eyes would think they walked separately the road to God, that they were distant and removed from one another. But if they had eyes of the spirit, they would see two hearts inseparably joined, two souls united in God. Whoever saw one would see the other more really than anyone with earthly vision would ever believe. That was the mystery of spiritual love, and Clare and Francis were proof of its existence. She wondered how many would have eyes to see.

After a few days, she moved to the church of San Angelo di Panzo. But as her soul was not fully at rest there, at the advice of the Blessed Francis she removed at last to the church of San Damiano.

Thomas of Celano

San Damiano

"*a* place for me." That is how she viewed the church of San Damiano. Once she was there, she could live apart from Francis and still be a part of his life. Before coming to San Damiano she felt so alone. Francis had his brothers, and wherever they were, he had a place to call home. The brotherhood *was* his home. She needed something like that, too.

Immediately after Francis had received her into the Order he took her to the Benedictine nuns of San Paolo near Bastia. A few days later she moved to another Benedictine convent, San Angelo di Panzo on the slopes of Mount Subasio. There she was joined by her sister Agnes, a girl of 15, who like Clare had run away from her home to give her life to God.

But Clare was not a Benedictine, and she felt alone and removed from the brothers. So she asked Francis for a home where she could live the new way of life he had given her. And Francis understood.

He begged the church of San Damiano from the Bishop of Assisi and gave it to Clare and Agnes so they would have a place on this earth where they could live the perfect poverty of Jesus Christ. Soon Clare and Agnes were joined by Pacifica, Benvenuta, Cecilia and Philippa. Clare was at peace, for now there was a sisterhood that was a home.

San Damiano was the small chapel where Francis had heard the voice of Christ from the crucifix, "Francis, go and repair my house which, as you see, is entirely in ruins." Francis had done as the Lord commanded. He restored this little church, prophesying as he did so that some day this would be the home of the Poor Ladies of the Lord.

How this fact filled Clare with joy! The home Francis had given her was the very place where his own call from God had begun. How well he had understood her request. This church was so much a part of him. Here he had worked in the sweat of his brow, begging stones in Assisi and mortaring them into place. Here in his fear he had hidden from his father's wrath, and here he had learned in prayer how to overcome fear and face his father.

In choosing this particular place he had given her a large part of himself. Yes, he had understood what she was asking. It was truly a place for her.

*Her union with him was so complete and har-
monious, her mind and heart so like his own, that
it is difficult to know how much was conscious
imitation on her part and how much natural en-
dowment.*

Lothar Hardick, O.F.M.

Pilgrims in Spirit

She had known almost at once that she would
follow him. The first time she heard Francis
preach, his words pierced her heart with love for
Jesus, and his soul was one with hers. She soon
learned that they could never be together, for then
they would not be free, they would not be who they
really were, two pilgrims in love with the Lord, two
souls who were closer apart than they could ever be
together. Together they might end up loving each
other more than the treasure they had found in one
another's heart.

She had heard the echo of her own voice in
Francis' words, and he had found in her the
incarnation of every word he spoke. They were
pilgrims in spirit, poor and wandering hearts in love
with God; and knowing they loved each other, they
were never lonely.

Clare drew her ideals from Francis' words, and
Francis, she felt, drew his words at times from the
inspiration of her life. She made it possible for him to
believe that what he spoke was livable, that the

gospel life brought joy indeed, and that every word that Jesus uttered could be lived by those who heard his words with open hearts.

Clare hoped that she would become the living proof of everything Francis believed in. And that was why she had to follow him the moment she heard him speak: They had been fashioned for each other out of the solitude of the ages. And they had known each other longer than they knew.

Sister and Brother Planets

though he had brought her to the Lord, Francis was not always on her mind. In fact she dwelled so much in God that Francis was seldom in her thoughts. And at the same time he was always in her thoughts. How this could be, Clare did not fully understand. She only knew that her real lover and beloved was the Lord and that Francis was intimately related to her love for Jesus. Her preoccupation was not with Francis, but with her Lord. She loved Francis, but was not dependent upon him as she had been at first.

How hard it had been in the beginning. The first time Clare understood that she and Francis could never be together she cried all night. She was only 17 at the time, and at that blessed time of youth so many things seem unfair which later prove to have been

12

providential. But it was not "later"; it was the full flowering of her adolescence. This made everything vague and unclear in her mind like the perpetual haze that lay over the valley of Spoleto. She only knew that she would love him forever and that their marriage of mind and heart was already a fact. Why she loved a man 12 years older than she when so many young men her own age sought her love, she never even considered; for she never thought of Francis' age. She just loved him.

Now she understood that they each had a mission to fulfill, and they moved in separate but concentric spheres that centered on the Lord. Their intimacy was not with each other but with God. Yet Clare never doubted that her closeness to the Lord effected a growing closeness to Francis. She understood, as Francis did, that preoccupation with each other would destroy the center and separate them from God and from each other, broken circles shooting crazily off into space.

But the center *would* hold, for they both uncompromisingly looked upon the Lord, she in prayer and contemplation at San Damiano and Francis everywhere upon the road. His orbit was wider than hers, reaching out to the length and breadth of Italy. Hers lay inside of his, drawing Francis to the center and holding her tightly between Francis and God himself. They were like sister and brother planets circling the Lord.

Clare always referred to herself as the "little plant" of the Blessed Francis, nourished with his spirit and guarded with his most tender solicitude; and she consciously strove to become like him in all things.

Lothar Hardick, O.F.M.

Roses

She loved flowers on the altar. Roses especially reminded her of who she was and of what she must become. They were so tight in the beginning, and then slowly, imperceptibly they opened up and surrendered themselves to whatever lay about them. Even in dying they dropped their petals gracefully; and if you listened quietly enough, you could hear the silence of their falling. All that was left was the center, naked and free of all the pampering satin petals it held so closely at the start. And the center held in perfect poverty.

Jesus

Jesus, always Jesus smoldering in her heart, then flaming up suddenly, surprising her with the ardor of his love. No matter how intensely she looked to Francis for teaching and guidance, for friendship and brotherhood, he never replaced Jesus as Lord and master of her heart and soul. And Jesus proved over and over again his love for her. Always, even when she was beginning to despair of his love, he would return suddenly, unexpectedly, the warmth of his entry as soft as the morning sun upon the white roses of her little garden. Her Lord always seemed to know when his seeming distance was causing havoc in her heart. She would turn inward and pray aloud in her anguish, begging Jesus to come to her and fill the void. And the Lord would remain silent and away.

Then, when she was not praying but working in her garden, or nursing her sick sisters, or working at her sewing, it would happen—with a sudden rush of warmth he would be there, saving her again, rewarding her patience with his presence and the power of his healing. And he would seem to come from within as if he had in fact been smoldering in her heart with just enough spark to be reenkindled by the Spirit—that Spirit like the wind, blowing where he would and refusing to be harnessed by any magic formula of prayer.

Slowly she learned to wait upon the Lord and his Spirit, to open her mind and heart like thirsty ground waiting for rain, like rose petals waiting for the sun. And if she waited in patience and continued to work faithfully at whatever was at hand, the Lord would always surprise her, sometimes meeting her in the kitchen, sometimes in the laundry, sometimes in the refectory, sometimes even when she was sweeping the earthen floor with nothing particular on her mind.

Waiting

From trying to pray well, Clare learned a lot about loving God. For one thing she learned that love involves an enormous amount of waiting. You waited for your beloved to come upon the mountain tops; you waited just for a glimpse of him bounding across the valley of your loneliness, and like a gazelle he was restless and seldom stayed long with you. And if you were too dependent on his visits, his tangible presence, then most of the time you felt lonely and frustrated, and your thoughts were preoccupied with the beloved and his next coming. And so you learned to live as independently of his felt presence as possible. You learned to expect little and to greet every visitation as a gift, a surprise that would happen when you least expected it.

You prayed for his coming, but you were wise not to let your longing, your loneliness interfere with living, with what had to be done from moment to moment. You kept giving even when you felt nothing in return. And most of all, you learned to trust your beloved, to know deep within that love did not depend on your experience of his presence. In fact, most of the time his love was a felt absence that prepared the heart for the ecstasy of meeting once again.

Life with Jesus was a drama of finding and losing, of separation and reunion. The price you paid for ecstatic union was the loneliness and heartache of continued separation, of wondering if he had abandoned you, had ceased loving you. With the Lord, Clare experienced at times the ecstatic union of mind and heart and soul and body; the intervals between his visitations caused her more pain than she cared to think about. She tried not to remember the intervals; they would, after all, continue to recur without her dwelling on them. She tried to live in the present, hoping and praying, but not depending too much on the coming of her beloved. And by living in the present Clare gradually learned that the contemplative life is not a living for ecstasy but a simple faith that knows the Lord is always present whether or not his presence is felt in any tangible way.

Clare was a vessel of humility, a shrine of chastity, a flame of love, the essence of kindness, the strength of patience, the bond of peace, and the source of loving unity in her community: meek in word, gentle in deed, lovable and beloved in all things . . . . In the lifetime of Clare the power of her holiness shone forth in many

different miracles. Thus she restored to one of the Sisters of her monastery the use of her voice, . . . to another, . . . she restored the power to speak correctly, . . . for another she opened her deaf ear so that she could hear. By making the sign of the cross over them, she freed others from fever . . . and other maladies.

Document of Canonization

Love

Does the love of God mean the end of human love for those who embrace the virginal life? Clare hoped her love for Francis, for his brothers, and for the Poor Ladies of San Damiano proved to everyone that her vow of chastity had made her warm and gentle and full of love for everyone whose life she touched.

Human love was for her the only way to divine love, for what in fact was the love of God if not for the Body of Christ? God had become human, and it was in this Body of his that he was to be found and loved. It was the human body which was the instrument of loving. One who withdrew from others was somehow frightened of people, deluded into believing that God was only spirit. God had indeed become human, flesh was now inspirited, and Clare treated people accordingly.

Francis realized the great faith she had in Christ's

presence in his Mystical Body. He was always
sending people to her, and she would lay her hands
on them and ask the Lord to heal them.

Cicadas

S he heard his name every day in the olive trees,
the cypresses and the low bushes surrounding
San Damiano. God, God, God! That is what the
chorus of cicadas seemed to be singing. They
reminded her of her Lord because she believed God
was singing through them as he sang through all of
creation. God's song was in everything because she
heard with ears of faith and because she strove to
love him without reservation of any kind.

To love the Lord with her whole heart and her
whole mind and her whole soul! That is what Clare
wanted above all else in life. Everything, including
Francis and his new way of life, was secondary to her
all-consuming desire to love the Lord, her God. He
was in her mind and in her heart, in her speech and
in her silence, in her work and in her rest, in her
waking and in her sleeping, in her eyes and ears and
mouth and nose and fingertips.

God, God, God! He was the secret of what she and
her Poor Ladies were all about. And the cicadas kept
reminding all of them that he was a song in the ears
of the believer, a melody in the heart.

She was the new woman of the Valley of Spoleto, who poured forth a new fountain of the water of life . . . .

Document of Canonization

A New Jerusalem

*t*hough Clare loved the Lord with her whole heart, Francis was also a part of that love. Sorting that out was not difficult because the two had always been associated in her mind. She had never loved God in the abstract but rather as she saw him incarnate in Francis. She had found God in Francis. Wherever one was, there was the other also. And she never thought this feeling divided her love.

Over the years Clare grew in the conviction that God was present to her in every person she met, and it all began with Francis in their little Eden of Assisi. That is why she loved Assisi so. Their love began there, the three of them: Francis, Clare and the Lord.

Before she was finally cloistered at San Damiano, Clare used to walk the streets of Assisi for hours, making every corner of the city her own. There were 11 gates to the city, and after she met Francis, she always viewed them as the gates of a New Jerusalem.

She and Francis together had been graced with the care of this new city that had descended from on high. Out of Assisi's gates would flow the living waters of Christ, and into Assisi would stream the chosen people of the new city. They would come to Assisi seeking the Lord who had been revealed anew in his servant Francis.

Clare believed that Assisi was a sacred city and that she and her Poor Ladies had been given a position on God's holy mountain second only to Francis himself. Somehow she sensed also that her name would be forever linked with that of Francis. They were "married" forever as the Adam and Eve of a new family in the Church of God.

The Lord had built for them a new Jerusalem called Assisi, and men and women from every corner of the earth would come there hoping that this new Eden was not just a dream, a fantasy spread by the idle tongues of travelers. And she knew they would not be disappointed. The lovers among them would understand why two shared her heart, why God chose a man *and* a woman to build his New Jerusalem, and why a pure and virginal love begets so many children in the Lord.

When she was yet a maiden in the world, she sought from a tender age to pass through this . . . world by the path of the pure and to guard the precious treasure of her virginity in unstained modesty . . . . Noble by birth, but more noble by her manner of life, she preserved above all under this holy Rule the virginity which she previously guarded so well.

Document of Canonization

Chastity

Somehow she was sure she was an important part of Francis' chastity. In loving her as he did, his love was turned toward a woman as chaste as he was, a woman who reminded him of Lady Poverty and the Blessed Virgin. Clare felt humble in thinking that, because it was true, and truth has nothing of pride in it.

She liked to think that when Francis was tempted, he would turn his thoughts to her and, in her, what was ugly became beautiful, what was evil became good. She dwelled apart from him, inaccessible in her vowed love, like an ideal woman one imagines will purify one's love, and somehow does.

She remembered Brother Angelo telling her of that night in the tower in Rome when Francis cried out that he was afraid to be alone, and Brother Angelo had stayed with him. And Clare hoped she was there, too, in his thoughts, her presence a shield against insomnia and fear. Francis would never be alone as long as she loved him, for love reached out from San Damiano, an embrace of spirit forever extended toward Francis and his brothers.

Words

Words! How important they had been to her from the first time she heard Francis preach, and especially from that Lent of her 18th year when Francis inspired her to leave her home and join him and his brothers at the Portiuncula. She had hung upon his every word as if his words were life itself.

Later she would listen to Francis preach and speak, and his words became God's words for her and her Ladies at San Damiano. And over the years, whenever he was troubled or in doubt Francis would send to Clare for her words. Her words were not only balm to his spirit, but he immediately acted upon them as spirit and life from the Lord.

In a way she did not fully understand, the Lord Jesus became tangible in their midst whenever they spoke together. They met, bringing from separate caves the Christ each had found in solitude, and the Word became flesh in their sharing him. He became the Lord of their union, and he was the same Christ each had found in the silence of prayer and penance.

Each was so intimately united in mind and heart with Christ that their union with each other was made perfect in him. At least, that is how Clare saw it, and she praised the Lord for the wonder of his gift to her through Francis.

She almost said to her *and* Francis, but that would not be true. From the very beginning the Lord had called her *through* Francis. He was the Lord's instrument, the voice God had used to call her out of her father's house into the new and wonderful world of the Spirit.

And by using Clare as his voice, God in his providence let her repay Francis. Once, for example, when Francis was in deep anxiety about his future, wondering whether he should retire from the life of apostolic preaching and devote himself entirely to prayer and contemplation, he sent Brother Masseo to Clare for her advice and counsel. She immediately went to one of her sisters, and they prayed together for God's answer. And while they prayed, both women heard deep in their hearts the same words: "I have not called Francis for his own sake alone, but that he may reap a harvest of souls and that many may be saved through him."

Brother Masseo later told Clare that her words were identical to those of Brother Sylvester, whom Francis had also consulted. Francis had received these words with great joy and immediately set out to preach to the people of God. Clare's own heart was filled with peace and joy at this news because she had become for Francis what he was for her, the word of the Lord!

Days of Heartache

*t*hen came the days of heartache and pain
when she felt Francis slowly moving away
from her and the other Poor Ladies of San Damiano.
At first he had come often to see them and to preach
to them the Good News of Jesus. Then, without
explanation, his visits grew less and less frequent and
finally stopped altogether.

Clare supposed it had something to do with
fidelity and Francis' deep inner need to be one and
undivided. But she could not understand how she
could bring division to his heart, for her own fidelity
to Christ and Francis' vision had been tested and
found true and unswerving.

Perhaps they saw each other differently. Francis
was everything she loved and dreamed of becoming;
he brought her happiness and joy. He led her
constantly to Jesus and made her love for the Lord
alive and glowing in the Spirit. Was she something
different to him? Did she come between him and the
Lord he loved so much?

If that were true, how ironic it would be, for she
then would be an instrument of evil for the man who
had brought her to God. How could a love as pure as
hers cause Francis such anxiety and make him so
unsure of himself? Perhaps that was it; her love was
pure and good and therefore like a magnet for
Francis. It drew him to her instead of to his Lord.

But that made no sense at all to Clare, for people
did just the opposite in her life: They led her closer

and closer to the God who had become incarnate in them. But then she realized how many things she and Francis did share, their deep fidelity to the Lord, and she knew this great difference between them was the price she would have to pay for being part of God's plan for Francis. And having said that to herself, she still didn't like it—and never would.

Contemplation

Clare sat quietly in her little garden and surrendered her senses to everything around her. It was like opening up to God himself, and this, she knew, was a part of contemplation. If you closed yourself up and feared your senses, then contemplation was impossible. She loved to sit in her garden and experience the fullness of creation through sight and sound and touch and smell, and even the taste of the breeze scented with ginestra and oleander, rosemary and myrtle.

Often she would rise at 4:00 a.m. and go out to her garden just to listen to the dawn. *Listen* was the right word because dawn meant the whole sky would be alive with swallows screaming crazily in the morning light. Swallows *were* morning in Assisi.

Sometimes, too, she would sit in the late afternoon and look up at Mount Subasio and remember the little cliff where she used to steal away as a child.

From there she could see the Rocca Maggiore with the ends of the city walls clinging to it as arms to a strong body. She loved her cliff, for there she could be alone and touch the earth, whisper back to the trees and inhale the spirit of the mountain.

And then there was Francis. No matter where he was, she could see him and hear him. She would feel again the touch of his hand in hers when she visited him as a young girl. She could still smell his frail body through the strong scent of sweat trapped in the wool of his habit.

His taste was that of the wilderness. As a young girl she used to pull out blades of grass or weeds and put them to her mouth, and whenever she saw Francis or talked to him that wild taste of plants and leaves and twigs filled her imagination. He was a

man who lived in the woods and slept in caves; he always had soil and grass clinging to his habit. She imagined his taste was more plant than animal.

Or maybe it was his gentleness and quietness that brought plants into her mind. There was nothing of animal fierceness in Francis. There was only courtesy and kindness and a delicate, gentle yet strong nature that reminded her of trees. Maybe that was why she used to hug trees when she was young and deeply in love with Francis. People would surely have thought her crazy, but her first love for Francis was as young as she was at the time. Whenever she was lonely or did not understand his distance and reserve, she would embrace a tree and feel comforted in some strange, inexplicable way.

All these memories and more were hidden away in her garden. Small as it was, it contained so much of what she needed for contemplation and intimacy, union with God and people and nature.

Camelot

to love Francis you had to love knighthood and chivalry as well. Though he had turned his back on war, he never ceased to be a courteous knight at heart. Everything he did spoke of chivalry and the knightly code, and to understand that was to understand in large part the marvelous little man whose very name reminded Clare of the troubadours.

As a girl, she, like Francis, had listened to the troubadours from Provence. She too had been captivated by their songs of Arthur and his knights. In some mysterious way she and Francis were a part of that story of King Arthur. Out of those childhood memories transformed now by the love of God, she and Francis walked into the real world, she the lady of the castle and he a knight upon the road.

No longer the fantasy of youth there was still, despite its earnestness, an element of play in this little drama that she and Francis were enacting for all the world to see. It was a tale of chivalry they were living, a new tale with Christ himself as the king and liege lord. There was also a new dimension of joy which Francis brought to the old chivalric ideals of total devotion to the lord, courtesy toward everyone and selfless compassion for the poor and weak.

Their love was unintelligible apart from Camelot, for that world of the Round Table explained the nobility of Francis and of Clare and made them different from other beggars of the time. They both lived in utter poverty, but their faces shone. Their bearing was such that everyone who met them saw who they really were beneath their peasant garb; their hands outstretched to beg somehow invited others to kneel and kiss a hidden royalty.

It was this element of chivalry that Clare loved most in Francis. Far from lowering her self-esteem, the poverty they shared made her feel like a true lady. This poverty was not penance or self-flagellation or gloomy asceticism. It was putting on the Lord Jesus Christ, who had emptied himself, taking the form of a servant. And who, wearing the garments of the great King himself, could look down upon himself or be ashamed?

In this new world of Francis and his lady, beggars could walk with pride and self-esteem, for they were heralds of the great King. And those who announce the good news of his coming do not walk around depressed, beating their breasts. They put on rags and raise their heads. And everyone with eyes to see rejoices that the countryside is once again peopled by lords and ladies whose court is a movable Camelot open to simple folk from every land on earth, a Camelot where every man and woman can put on the royal robes of Lady Poverty and walk again with pride.

Swords in the Sunlight

*t*he Kingdom! Always the Kingdom and its upbuilding! The discipline of her life, her penance, her poverty—these were heroic because she would be a lady, a spouse of Christ the King. She would do at home the great deeds Francis did upon the road. She would not be outdone, for she, too, was noble and fine, a lady fit for a great knight like Francis. Together they would shine that the Lord

Jesus might be glorified.

Clare, from the beginning, recognized the heroic in everything she and Francis did. They grew into adulthood, but they never left that part of adolescence which kept them ever faithful to their ideal. What they did was hard, but it was a hardness that shone, a hardness that polished the soul.

It polished the soul because it was all for the love of Jesus and the building of his Kingdom, and the cost was never too high. It was all for him who had been crucified for them. Clare knew that the life of a lady in this new Kingdom was the daily carrying of the cross, but it was a task that was noble and fine because the wood of her cross was cut from the cross of Jesus, her Lord and King. And if you carried that cross, your life gradually acquired a new dignity. You experienced a new freedom and your step began to lighten.

Clare noticed especially that her cross slowed her down so she could see more along the way. You couldn't hurry when you were carrying a cross. You began to notice the stones beneath your feet. You saw the pain in the eyes of those you passed and how important it was to them that you bear your cross like a true lady. They were encouraged seeing your cheerfulness and the light in your eyes; and they also looked up the road to see where you were going with such grand determination. You were building the Kingdom all along the way, and if you dared look back, you would see a multitude following you, their crosses gleaming like swords in the sunlight.

She was the princess of the poor, the duchess of the humble, the mistress of the chaste, the abbess of the penitent . . . . Her very life was for others a school of instruction and doctrine. In this book of life the others learned the rule of life; in this mirror of life the others beheld the path of their own life.

Document of Canonization

A Sense of Belonging

In those who came to her at San Damiano, Clare saw women who were searching for someone and something to belong to. The something was a sisterhood with common goals and ideals, and the someone was Christ the Lord. Before they came, they had been a part yet not a part of their families and friends. There was something inside calling them away, calling them to solitude and prayer.

Even among those who loved them these women felt somehow different and not really at home. To marry and settle down was too confining to them; to live alone was unthinkable. In coming to Clare they realized a new sense of belonging. At San Damiano their deepest needs would be met by God and by the other Poor Ladies, and they would be able to give freely of the love within them. They would be in a place where God came first, where life was simple, where there were others with whom they could share their love of God.

A Kingdom of the Heart

Jesus. How much that name meant to her! It summoned up everything she wanted in life. So many people in Assisi were busy and anxious, acquiring and building up little perishable kingdoms that consumed most of their energy. And still they were unhappy. But with the simple sound of Jesus' name in her heart Clare could summon up her own kingdom, a kingdom of the heart where her Lord dwelt and where he would reign forever.

It was difficult for Clare to understand how anyone could really abandon this inner kingdom for superficialities and transient pursuits. But she realized, too, that Jesus was a gift. Not everyone had enjoyed the privilege of her background and her friendship with a prophet of the Lord like Francis.

But did they not know their own emptiness and seek to fill it with something more than ceaseless talk and busyness and the inflation of their own selves? Surely they did. And that is why she repeated Jesus' name over and over again. She was asking him to send Francis' brothers to the ends of the earth with the message that Jesus fills, Jesus satisfies, Jesus answers those questions people are afraid to ask.

Clare saw herself and all her Poor Ladies as the virgins of a new temple that would draw the whole world to Assisi as to a new oracle. There God had spoken a unique message reaffirming the incarnation of his Son and setting a new sun in the sky in the person of Francis. The dawn that was Francis would be a turning point in human movement toward perfection and union with God.

On what future mountaintop would mind and heart unite to draw people finally and inevitably to their destiny? And what new prophet would complete what Francis was here continuing? Jesus! Would it not be Jesus returning who would stand on the last mountaintop, drawing all the earth to himself? Where that would be didn't matter, really. It would be wherever Jesus set his foot. And all the gods of every time and place would dwell in a temple inhabited by a triune God, for all the divine creations of every civilization were partial revelations snatched from God's whispers to those who tried to hear him. In the end his full voice would stand embodied upon the final pinnacle of space and time. That is what Clare prayed for every time she summoned up in mind and voice that alpha and omega, Jesus Christ!

*There were times when he was afraid he was too
reserved in his attitude toward her and that he
stood at too great a distance from her. But she
never disappeared completely from his thoughts.
She was the perfect fulfillment of his dream and
his holy task.*

Auspicius van Corstanje, O.F.M.

To Love From Afar

Clare eventually understood the distance at
which Francis kept her and why. Very
simply, he loved her. Therefore she threatened his
all-consuming love for God. She didn't, of course;
but Francis thought she did because he was afraid
not of her but of himself. She had seen the same thing
in others; they seemed to be afraid of someone or
something when it was only themselves they feared.
Clare knew, in fact, that no one understood the
singleness of Francis' love for Jesus better than she
did. And no one would more faithfully protect that
love than she.

But because Francis was the kind of man he was,
he could never allow anyone, even her, to rest even
in the corner of his eye. His eyes were fixed entirely
on the Lord. If he saw you in looking on the Lord,
that was wonderful. But if he saw you between him
and God or was distracted by glimpsing you out of
the corner of his eye, then he would run away and
beg the Lord's forgiveness for his "unfaithfulness."

36

Sometimes, though he was older, she felt like scolding him for being so childish. But then she would remember that he *was* a child—and scolding might make him grow up. It was, after all, the child in him that made him so lovable, so different from the grim, so-called saints she had heard about in childhood stories.

But what was she going to do with such an impossible man whose single-hearted love of God left no room for her? Or if it did, it was so carefully concealed it took an inner eye to see it? What could she do with this saint who had brought her here to San Damiano and then seemingly forgotten her in his interminable journeys preaching Jesus Christ crucified?

What could she do, after all, except love God and let Francis be free and never let on how much it hurt her that he saw her nearness as an obstacle to his love for God? She would love him from afar, and she would thereby be near in a way that did not frighten him.

The Power of Prayer

h ow she had struggled with her heart during those months after she heard Francis preach in San Rufino's and San Giorgio's. It was difficult to explain, even years later, the mesmerizing effect he had on her. And what made it even more difficult for her, she knew then as she knew now, Francis was praying for her.

That is what made his preaching so different from others'. He not only preached the word of God, but he took the responsibility for his words and became involved with the people to whom he preached. One way he did this was to pray incessantly that the word God spoke through him would penetrate the souls of his hearers and change their lives.

And so Clare had been swept away both by Francis' preaching and by the intercessory power of his prayer. She felt helpless and dizzy inside as wave after wave of God's grace washed over her. Every time she tried to stand up a new wave would hit her, and she could feel herself weakening in her struggle with God.

All along Clare knew that if she would only surrender, she would float easily in the immensity of God's love. But floating meant letting go of too many things she loved and clung to for her to surrender easily. There was her family first of all, the love and tenderness of her parents and the affection and closeness she felt for her sisters. Other things, too, were good and beautiful to her. Her young heart found it difficult to understand why anyone should have to turn loose of them to follow a Christ who himself proclaimed the goodness of all creation and the love of his Father for everything he had made, even for the nervous little sparrows who clung so close to the earth though they could fly.

But Francis continued to pray, and in the end he and his God won. Together they were too much for her, a lesson she never forgot in all the ensuing years when she prayed for others. When you prayed, you were never alone. It was you and God together entering into the very depths of the person for whom you prayed. And though the person might at first sense your entry as an invasion, ultimately it was your forceful entry that broke down the doors of fear and hatred imprisoning the heart.

Over and over again surrender brought freedom and release of pent-up frustrations and longings for love. There in the core of the other, you and God would take up residence, and the person would experience true love for the first time. And another pray-er would begin to join with God in assaulting the yet unvanquished hearts of countless ailing members of Christ's Body.

All of this and more she learned while struggling with herself and God and other people. And like any woman in love she never forgot her first lessons in love, her first knowledge of the ways of her beloved.

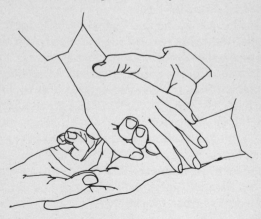

*They discovered in each other the same luxury of
God's presence and the same fire that consumed
all the idols in their hearts, until they were ash.*

Auspicius van Corstanje, O.F.M.

A Vacancy for God

"**F**or the love of my Lord and Savior Jesus
Christ!" How often and with what
fervor Francis repeated that phrase!
Clare understood much of Francis from his love of
chivalry, but his love for Jesus Christ crucified
opened up his real being. He was a man in love with
his Lord. No person or thing would ever detract
from his love, from his single-hearted devotion to
Christ. When you love a man like that, you know
from the very beginning that you must take, at most,
second place in his heart. Even chronologically
Clare came after the Lord in Francis' life. He was
already deeply in love with Jesus when she came into
his life, and he already had brothers whom he loved.

It is hard to love a man whose focus is wholly
elsewhere, who views you at best as a co-worker in
the Kingdom of his Lord. But Clare grew to
understand and accept Francis and to love him no
less because he would never love her as she loved
him. And she, too, was in love with the Lord. That
they had in common, and that love of God would
never change.

She only wished they could work more closely

together for the Lord. What was it that separated men and women in the Kingdom? Why did they have to work apart rather than together? Or did they really work together though apart?

She only knew that she would never abandon Francis. No matter how far he roamed or how long he stayed away, Clare would always faithfully love him. She would never abandon him as the Lord never abandoned her. That was what she knew of love: The Lord was faithful and would not leave his people. And Clare, participating in his love, would remain faithful to her loves as well, for that was what she knew of love.

She saw Francis' fidelity in everything he did and in his constant refrain, "for the love of my Lord and Savior Jesus Christ." No matter how engaged Francis was with any other activity or how ardently he worked with or loved the people of God, he always left room at the center of his heart for God. He left a vacancy for God that only God could occupy. There in that open space in her own heart she also met God. She, too, always left a vacancy for him. But when the Lord came to dwell there, he brought Francis with him, and Clare's spirit joined with Francis' in praising God.

The love of their Lord and Savior Jesus Christ secured that vacancy in the center of their hearts and made possible their love for one another. God is love and those who love him remain somehow in one another. Clare and Francis would remain united forever, for the center of their love was the eternal God.

A Faithful God

Clare noticed as she grew older that she was slowly becoming what she had always dreamed of being; she was slowly, imperceptibly realizing the potential within her through the action of God. Everything that had happened to her through the years she now saw as a part of God's plan for her. Even her pain and frustration over Francis had been good for her.

It was a matter of trust and believing at first. Once you had persevered, it was a matter of seeing that what you hoped could happen, was in fact happening all along. You grew into that fullness which is Christ, and you knew that God was indeed faithful to his word.

Such growth comes to those who believe an inner voice, those with hope for the future, those who love when all is still a promise unfulfilled. Faith, after all, is where it all begins. In faith, you believe that God loves you, and you are made good by his creative loving. And only he who first believed in you really makes it possible for you to believe in yourself. You live and love in the stormy, unrealized present, clinging to the glimpse of the future given by hope. Eventually, the dream you believed, the future you hoped in becomes the present, and suddenly you see clearly that it is all realized from moment to moment. When you are aware of the future, open to its presence, the present *is* the future.

God was accomplishing something new in the

world through Francis and Clare, and they had both dared to believe it when it still wore the vague colors of a dream.

Rainy Days

*t*here were days when the rains would come and settle in over the whole Valley of Spoleto. But rain never depressed her. On the contrary, it was a source of encouragement, because Clare knew that somewhere out there on the side of Mount Subasio Francis was burrowing into a small cave where he would rediscover the love of God within himself and pray intently over it until the skies cleared. He would emerge renewed and ready to share the newly found treasure with others.

True, she worried about the physical pain and suffering Francis endured in all those damp caves, but she knew he would never change the pattern of penance in his life. So identified was he with the poor, suffering Christ that he considered every pain and deprivation a privilege, an opportunity to share in the sufferings of his Lord.

Clare understood that kind of love because it was in her as well. She, however, suffered not only with her Lord, but with Francis, and she knew in some strange, intuitive way when Francis was suffering. Rain was only one reminder among many. She knew and loved Francis so well that there was an invisible bond of communication between them that was continually carrying felt messages to and fro. Love was that real to Clare, and what she heard and understood in prayer was not that different an experience from what she heard and understood intuitively from Francis. Love made both experiences possible, and it explained why the language of lovers and mystics was the same. She thought that rain, too, might be something she had in common with other lovers.

Tilting at the Empty Air

a time for us. There never will be time for us, thought Clare. An edge of bitterness crept into her heart. Giving, always giving, always loving a God who seemed so far away. Always looking toward some future union with the Lord while the present was filled with sacrifice and privation. All the while, she and Francis lived apart like two souls under some kind of spell that prevented their meeting, that allowed them no time together. Was it too much to ask for a few hours with Francis, for the simple sound of his voice to lift her heart and rekindle her spirit, to rest one hour with him by her side? Was a loving God so terribly forbidding, or was it misguided man who made it so?

Clare knew these thoughts were vain and foolish and full of self-pity, but she sometimes was overwhelmed by Francis' singleness of heart and by his great fear of loving her lest he steal the affection of his Lord's bride. To Francis she belonged wholly to God, and as such was so sacred and holy that were he even to look at her with affection, he would be profaning his Lord's love. Clare understood that, but sometimes she felt Francis carried it too far and made of God some blind and jealous king who hoarded his wives and flew into a rage if anyone but looked at one of them. Surely, God was not like that.

Francis lived in some ideal chivalric world, riding about Umbria on the white charger of chastity, tilting at the empty air. That, of course, made him even more lovable, and Clare would feel more frustrated than ever. For who could resist a man as pure as Francis? Who could fail to succumb to his otherworldly sense of honor and devotion to his Lord? He was a knight of the Great King, and the women of San Damiano were his Lord's gentle ladies living in a lovely white tower he was unworthy to enter. So he continued to ride the roads of the world, fighting the battles of his Lord and righting the wrongs of the Kingdom. And if by chance he passed the shining tower of San Damiano, he would salute it reverently from the plain, his heart filled with a holy reverence that made Clare weep for so idyllic a love.

For both of them, Jesus was their first and greatest love. They loved him in each other, just as he revealed his love separately in each of them.

Auspicius van Corstanje, O.F.M.

No One on the Road

The hardest time for Clare was when she expected Francis to visit her, and he didn't come. The brothers would assure her he was coming, and she would set her heart on it and rehearse over and over in her mind how it would be. She would wait for him like a child waiting wide-eyed for her father to return. And there would be no one on the little road to San Damiano! Then she would pack up her heart once again and try not to cry. And she would wonder how he could do it, because she knew that he understood what his failure to appear did to her.

How great was Francis' detachment that even with all the pain he knew his absence caused her, he would stay away! Surely God did not demand so much. But then Francis never waited for demands. His love for God was a free and total response to a God who had given himself to man in a perfect sacrifice of love. And so Francis, too, must render a perfect sacrifice to his God.

Clare understood only too well that she was that sacrifice, or at least a large part of it. That made it intelligible for her, but it never made her own

sacrifice easy. It would have been different had her vocation come directly from God with no intermediary, as Francis' had. But Francis had been the instrument God used to lead her to himself, and therefore Francis was an essential part of her life in the Lord. She longed to hear him speak of Jesus; she longed to hear once again the Spirit speaking through this little man as she had as a young girl. Especially as she grew older, she wanted to hear again God's word from her father and friend. His silence and his absence from her grew more terrible as the years wore on.

Because of Francis' withdrawal, she threw herself more and more upon the Lord, and found in him the lover Francis refused to be. Perhaps that was what Francis intended all along. Perhaps his seeming madness was the sanest thing he could do to complete the work God had begun in her. She wanted to believe that, too, because then everything seemed to make sense again. Jesus became her all, and Francis moved farther and farther into the background. He was always there, of course, but Jesus took his place in her heart, and she knew that only he was faithful. Only he would never fail her, only he could fill the emptiness in her heart.

Choosing God's Will

*Y*ou choose your vocation in life over and over again. It is not a decision made once for all time when one is young. Clare chose her life at San Damiano again and again, and each time she embraced the life of poverty she did so for slightly different reasons. As she grew in experience and in understanding of her commitment, she had to say yes again and again to a way of life that was not exactly the life she expected at the beginning.

She never knew, for example, how hard it would be to give up the love and companionship of her family until those dark days and nights when God seemed to have abandoned her and the original enthusiasm of serving the Lord died out. She knew then that the honeymoon of her relationship with God was over and that she had to rededicate herself to her heavenly spouse, a spouse different from the one she had originally imagined.

Her life with Francis, too, turned out different from what she had thought it would be. In the enthusiasm of her 18th year she had thought they would be together in the service of the Lord, that she and other Poor Ladies would go about the countryside with Francis and his brothers, caring for them and supporting them like the women in the Gospel who accompanied Jesus on the road and who were so much a part of his life on earth. How different that all turned out! She saw less of the brothers than anyone, and she remained in the monastery of San Damiano all her life.

What an adjustment that was! She had to recommit herself to a presence in the world totally other than the one she had once dreamed of. Her presence to Francis and his brothers was only in prayer; her journey involved no road but that which leads into the heart. She who had bargained for the contemplative *and* apostolic life and who longed to travel to Morocco as a missionary remained a cloistered contemplative;* but in embracing her life as God slowly revealed it to her, she ended up an apostle in a way she never envisioned for herself and her Poor Ladies.

God himself chose the manner of your witness. In

---

*"Clare and her sisters lived a cloistered life (certainly from 1219 on) since the rule prescribed this in strict terms. However, the sources of her life tell us that they did not always abide by it, thus revealing the existence of another way of living at San Damiano . . . .

"Celano as well as the sisters of San Damiano note in the process of canonization certain liberties regarding the cloister: it was open to persons who did not share the life of the monastery, to the Friars Minor: to the brothers who begged (C. 61), to Brother Stephen who was cured by Clare and who slept in the monastery (C. 32), and Clare herself on her deathbed 'desired the presence of priests and of holy brothers' (C. 45). Brother Juniper went to San Damiano. Sometimes the account of cures teaches us that certain sick people were in the cloister (C. 33, Process IV and IX, 6). There is also an account of a meeting between Clare and Francis at the Portiuncula . . . .

"The details related above as well as certain accounts and witnesses prove her great freedom compared to the orientation adopted by Hugolin in behalf of the first Poor Clares. They also highlight her personal conception regarding the imitation of Christ and her faithfulness to this conception." Heribert Roggen, *The Spirit of St. Clare* (Chicago, Franciscan Herald Press, 1971), pp. 76-79.

embracing his will, you discovered a self you did not know you could be, you discovered a part of yourself you would never have known in pursuing your own will alone.

To be open and sensitive to God's will! How difficult that was, because it meant accepting change and reembracing your emerging self. You always wanted to stop at some lower level because no matter how difficult the ascent, once you arrived there, you could relax and be comfortable. But then God would call again, and if you wanted to grow, you would have to let go of your comfort and risk a further climb.

When Summer Comes
and the Roses are in Bloom

a story was told in Assisi which, though it was not true, did capture something of what she and Francis suffered. Clare loved the story from the very first time she heard it because it was filled with sympathy and understanding and because it contained one of those delightful little miracles that were so much a part of the lives of the saints which she had heard as a young girl.

It seems that one winter's day she and Francis were on the road from Spello to Assisi. (Already a folk legend was surrounding them, for they had

never walked that road together!) It was a walk
people said the Lady Clare dearly loved because it
wound through the Valley of Spoleto. Even now as it
lay covered with fresh snow, it was more beautiful
than any landscape she knew. She and Francis were
both depressed, and the cold seemed to cut through
their rough clothes more bitterly than when they had
left Assisi earlier that day.

Clare suspected that they were both thinking the
same thing, that their low spirits resulted from what
had happened along the way. They had knocked on
several doors to beg for bread and water; and though
the kind peasants had generously given them food,
Clare and Francis noticed the suspicion and
disapproval in their eyes. They had also heard
several unpleasant insinuations which, even though
full of laughter and good cheer, had hurt them. They
walked in silence, night falling quickly around them.

Suddenly Francis broke the silence: "Lady, you
heard what the people were saying about us." A great
lump lay in her throat, and she could not answer. She
was afraid that if she tried, she would start crying.
They walked on in the tense silence.

Finally, Francis said haltingly, "We have to walk
apart, Clare. You can be back at San Damiano
before it is dark. I'll follow you at a distance, so you
won't be afraid."

His words were too much for her, and she sank to
her knees in the road. She knelt there with her face in
her hands, and then suddenly stood up and started
down the road with her head bowed. She forced
herself not to look back.

The road turned into the forest, and Clare could

feel the rapid beating of her heart as she neared the forest's edge. She felt she was leaving him forever, and she could not face that kind of future without some word of comfort and hope. She stopped and turned and cried out in a broken voice, "Francis, when will we see each other again?" Francis answered gently, "When summer comes and the roses are in bloom."

Then Clare stood open-mouthed and trembling. For from the snow-covered tops of bushes and small trees, roses began to appear in full bloom. Clare opened her arms and walked hesitantly to a small bush. She picked the roses tenderly, filling the folds of her habit with blossoms. She turned and walked back to Francis and let the roses fall through his open hands onto the clean white snow. From that day on they were never really separated again, though they saw each other seldom. Though the years came and went, the roses in her garden bloomed every summer for her and her Francis. *

How truly and innocently the legend-makers had understood! Clare hoped the story would survive the ages and that it would be told around the fire to every son and daughter of Assissi.

---

*This legend is to be found in Arnaldo Fortini, *Nova Vita Di San Francesco D'Assisi* (Milano, 1926), pp. 223-224.

A Mirror of Your Own Soul

Clare knew that Francis was secure in her love, and she was sure that made all the difference in his life. Whenever he was plagued with doubts, or the brothers did not understand, or God seemed far away, he could turn to her and know that she was there, constant in her love and devotion to him. Because of that simple fact Clare was more a part of his life than anyone. It was not their nearness to one another that mattered ultimately, but love—a love that never failed, a love that said "forever."

She knew Francis was a man of enormous detachment who would never consciously seek security, but he was also a man who accepted everything in his life as a gift from his Father. And because he knew her love was forever, he enjoyed a security which he had not sought out or even expected. It was a gift from his Father in heaven for which he was reverently grateful, a gift which made all his other detachments easier and enabled him to believe in himself and love himself. For after all, what man, even a saint, would not be more a man and more a saint with a woman's love to affirm him?

That thought comforted Clare. Her love for Francis placed her at the very heart of Francis' life and of the new movement in God's Church that he had founded. It was the bond between the Order of Friars Minor and the Order of Poor Ladies. But what she and Francis had was a gift, and not everyone would or could have that kind of relationship. Some, too, would deny that they needed such a relationship or even that it was good for their own spiritual health. Perhaps that was so. All she knew was that she was good for Francis and he for her. Like love itself, it was a mystery and could only be reverenced and appreciated, never really understood.

What a gift it is to find another person whose soul is a mirror of your own, someone with whom love and understanding is inevitable, someone whose fidelity is assured from the outset by the oneness you experience in the Lord!

Hearing of the now famous name of Francis, . . . Clare at once desired to hear and see him. She was moved thereto by the Father of spirits (Heb 12:9), whose first promptings each had followed though in different ways. And no less did Francis, impressed by the fair fame of so gracious a maiden, desire to see and speak with her . . . .

Thomas of Celano

Cast in the Same Mold

She and Francis were made of the same stuff. Instinctively and intuitively they had understood one another and were closer than anyone really knew. In fact, Francis told Clare that the first time they talked he felt that they had known each other all their lives. She had responded by saying that they had been born for each other, that Francis' dream would be her own. She spoke then with the enthusiasm of a 17-year-old girl, but her words had been prophetic.

They were made of the same stuff, these two: Francis never for an instant swerving from his determination to live the gospel life as literally as possible, and Clare equally determined to live the ideal God had shown her. Somehow it was easier for each of them to live that ideal because they were living it together. They never had to take their destiny and their love to the Lord for him to

approve. He was there at the beginning, at the very heart of their adventure.

Their love, especially, was not something they had apart from Jesus. He was the source and end of their love for one another. Clare felt that Jesus loved her when Francis loved her and that she loved Jesus when she loved Francis. Francis felt it too because they were cast in the same mold and they recognized the same hand in their making.

It is no wonder that the prayer of Clare was so powerful against the malice of men, when it angered even the demons. A certain devout woman of the diocese of Pisa once came to the monastery to give thanks to God and Saint Clare because through her merits she had been freed from five demons.

Thomas of Celano

A Young Woman's Story

Francis had no hold, no power over Clare because she loved him. Ironically, it is only those we despise who have a hold on us, those who have caused us some deep hurt that we cannot forgive. We return to them over and over again, and they torture us and poison our other relationships. They make us suspicious and fearful, and we cannot trust others. Clare had seen this quirk of human nature repeated many times in those who came to her for healing. They were tortured in mind and soul by memories that festered like a terrible disease, wearing down their spirit and weakening their bodies. Forgiveness and love—these were the only solution.

She remembered one young woman in particular who later became one of the Poor Ladies at San Damiano. Under the guise of freeing her from her fears, a man of her village had seduced her and, under the deception of true love, had lain with her.

Over and over again the girl tried to understand what had happened. She tried to believe the man had really loved her. She tried to believe that in his love for her he had been carried away by his own passion. She tried to believe that he was in fact trying to show her that sex was good and beautiful. But always the dark force of hatred came between her and her endeavor to understand. Fear raised its ugly head as well. She feared men and what they would do to her if they grew close to her, if she dared love them.

Clare heard her story with sympathy and pity, and she thought of her own relationship with Francis. How gentle, how reverent he had always been. That he loved her deeply, she had no doubt; and yet Francis was never overcome by passion.

Clare listened to the girl's story for over a year. She let the girl tell her story again and again in all its perceived horror and ugliness until one by one her demons were exorcised and she could let go of them, until she could forget by remembering in a forgiving cartharsis.

And in repeating her story she finally saw

everything in a new light. She saw her own blame as well. She saw that in spite of her innocence, she had not really been seduced; because of her own needs and insecurities, she had let things happen which she, too, had wanted to happen. That was the real reason she hated herself.

The Pain of Separation

Only those who have been in love know the pain and suffering involved in separation. Whether loss comes by death, distance or voluntary renunciation, the hurt is deep and the process of grieving complex. Clare was separated from Francis both by distance and by a renunciation which was a very real kind of death even though she had chosen to live apart for the sake of her Lord and Savior, Jesus Christ. And what hurt most of all was that the love never stopped. The heartache lay always deep within, at that level where dreams are made and nightmares raise their ugly heads. From time to time the terrible ache would surface; the dream God had shown her through Francis would turn to nightmare and she would tremble.

Clare was, after all, a woman, not some angelic presence who was ill at ease here on earth. Somehow this humble earth was the place for love, and any love she might know in heaven she would have to

59

take there with her.

Oh, Francis! How could she love him well enough to transcend the earth that lay heavy in her heart? How was she to lift the earth to heaven, or should she, could she? Perhaps you brought heaven to earth instead, perhaps you made of earth a heaven. The Word had become flesh, and from that event Clare took consolation and hope that a heavenly love, a spiritual love became flesh as well, in that love was always human no matter how much of the spirit was in it. And because it was human, love that involved separation always hurt; and the promise of the Kingdom, as real as that was, only made the hurt bearable and intelligible. It never took the hurt away.

Oh, Francis! How could she love him well enough to make their love eternal? The answer came, not in loving Francis, but in loving God more intensely. What happened over the years is that her love of God superseded her love for Francis, and she lived more and more in the presence of that Lord who had given her Francis as her friend and brother here on earth. But from the Lord, too, she was separated, except in spirit. So the two loves of her life mirrored each other and merged into one. She waited for both her beloveds as her reward in the Kingdom of heaven, as her part of her Lord's promise. And she met them both and was present to them every day only in prayer, that ever faithful nurturer of true love. Prayer made her loves eternal.

It was not long before the fame of the sanctity of the virgin Clare spread to nearby regions and from all sides women ran to the odor of her ointments . . . . All wished in holy rivalry to follow Christ; and desired to be made partakers of this angelic life which shone forth through Clare!

Thomas of Celano

Living in the Lord

"*W*hat am I doing with my life?" How often Clare had heard that question from women young and old, sometimes in great hope but more often in despair. She always answered by offering them an adventure in loving, a rich treasure she had found in a poor little field named Francis. It was a treasure which had grown and multiplied by the work of the Spirit at San Damiano. There life was simple but very rich and rewarding for those who entered into that bold experiment of living whole-heartedly the poverty of Jesus Christ. To those who could not join her at San Damiano, Clare opened up the treasure of the life they were already living and showed them how full of meaning any life was when lived in the Lord.

What struck her most about all of those who came to her was the infinite care and love that God had for each one. No matter what had happened in their lives or how dark life seemed to them. Clare could see God's providence in the pattern of their years.

It was Francis, however, whom Clare loved above all others. Her own sanctity and clarity of spiritual vision seem to have enabled her to penetrate more deeply than anyone else into the mystery of his extraordinary holiness, and with the miracle of the stigmatization her reverence must have increased immeasurably.

Lothar Hardick, O.F.M.

La Verna

One night when the moon was full and bright over the Valley of Spoleto, Clare reached out and held Francis in her soul. He was away to the north at the time on a lonely mountain called La Verna and she felt his loneliness and pain. He became somehow tangible to her, as if he were there reaching out to her in her cell.

He rested heavy on her mind, and she felt the heat of his cauterized eyes pulsing softly in the darkness. Her silent grief began dropping in tears onto the floor. Somehow this moment was more real to her than if Francis were really there. In this imagining her whole cell was flooded with light and air while their two souls floated lightly between the moonbeams that held this vision through the night.

Francis' soul seemed so light to her, so small and frail, so different from the power that flowed from him in daylight as he preached or walked magnetically through the streets of Assisi. He always said how small and wretched he was, that in him God had chosen to work through the lowliest of creatures. And now as she held his spirit in her imagination, she knew that it was true. How could this tiny, gentle man, so vulnerable, so sensitive, radiate such power?

And then shortly before dawn she suddenly felt as if a flame had touched her. The spirit within her fragile frame burned with a love hot as a seraph, and she experienced the entry of the living God. Francis far to the north on Mount La Verna was sealed with the wounds of Christ, and it was morning.

A Song for Her

*t*he whole world was present to her at San Damiano. The closer she grew to the one who is love in her small garden there, the more all of creation opened up to her. Clare marveled at how well she knew Mount Subasio simply from so many hours of looking at it in the distance. It had entered inside her and become a part of the way she saw all trees and every mountain. The more intimate her union with God became, the closer she seemed to be to nature, to the other Poor Ladies, and to Francis and his brothers. All these intimacies were somehow one and inseparable.

In the beginning she had feared (though she

couldn't admit it then) that the love of God would
divide and separate her other loves. In a sense it had,
perhaps because she expected it. But as she grew
older and persevered in prayer, she experienced at
the deepest level of her being a coming together, a
centering of love. She dared to believe that in loving
the Lord she had broken through to a more perfect
love of nature and of people.

Sometimes, for example, she would be praying
before the crucifix, and lifting her eyes to the
crucified, she would see the face of someone else. At
first this experience had frightened her because she
thought her love for people might be greater than her
love for Christ. Then one day when one of the

brothers was preaching in San Damiano, she looked at his face and saw there the face of Jesus. The two had become inseparably joined for Clare.

And she experienced something of God's Spirit in the life of trees and flowers. The force that drove the flowers up into sunlight drove her to lift up her heart and mind in prayer.

Over the years Clare had wondered if Francis felt this way too, and she prayed that God would reveal this to her before Francis died. The answer came when Clare least expected it. Francis was visiting her at San Damiano in the spring of 1225 when suddenly his eye sickness worsened. As a result he had to stay there for over 50 days in a little cell in the chaplain's house next to the monastery. Clare herself ministered to him, applying herbal lotions to his eyes, but nothing seemed to help. Even the light of a candle caused him unbearable pain, so his cell was always darkened.

One night when he was plagued more than ever by pain and sleeplessness, Francis began to feel sorry for himself. He cried out to the Lord to help him bear his suffering patiently. And the Lord answered him, promising him in exchange for his present pain an everlasting treasure beyond all his dreams.

The next morning Francis composed his Canticle of the Creatures and set it to music. Clare heard this song with amazement and with a new understanding of Francis. He who could not bear the light of the sun praised the Lord first of all through the sun; he who could not bear the candlelight praised God through Brother Fire who is beautiful and gay, full of power and strength! Clare understood then how close

Francis was to creatures. He had chosen this
creature world as his instrument of praise of the
Father. And she knew in her heart that he saw her
face in Sister Moon for he had dubbed the moon
bright and precious and fair—words which Brother
Leo once told her Francis used in describing Clare
herself.

Then Francis did one of those things which she
had come to expect from him. He immediately
dictated another canticle with words and music for
her and all her Ladies at San Damiano, a canticle full
of the wise teachings he had always given them:

> Listen, little poor ones called by the Lord,
> Who have been gathered together from
>   many parts and provinces:
>
> Live always in truth,
> That you may die in obedience.
>
> Do not look at the life outside,
> For that of the Spirit is better.
>
> I beg you in my great love for you,
> That you use with discretion the alms
>   which the Lord gives you.
>
> Those who are weighed down with sickness,
> And you others who are wearied by the care
>   of them,
> You should all of you bear it in peace,
> For you will see that such fatigue is very
>   precious.
>
> For you will each be a Queen crowned in
>   heaven

with the Virgin Mary
Through the merits of the mother Clare.
                              So be it. Amen

Clare heard these words with tears in her eyes, for
they told her that Francis knew what she was
thinking and was answering her question. He turned
her attention from him back to the Spirit inside,
hinting at how he saw her and each of the Poor
Ladies of San Damiano: They were mirrors of the
Virgin Mary herself. And further, so unlike him, he
had singled her out as mother of all her sisters. What
he felt for her would not be left unsaid until eternity.
And Clare turned in wonder to her garden and to
Mount Subasio and to prayer before the crucifix of
San Damiano.

Called by Name

She had always observed Francis. For as long
as she could remember Clare had known
Francis from afar, had watched him walking or
running or dancing through the streets of Assisi.
When she finally began talking seriously with him, it
was as if she were talking to someone she had known
all her life. They seemed to share the deepest part of
mind and heart from the very start of their
relationship. And Clare was cast under Francis' spell

the moment he began to talk with her and share his heart's dreams.

That was why she found it difficult at first to understand how Francis could so easily part from her and seemingly forget her in his absorption in the Lord. They would share on the very deepest level, and then Francis with a smile on his face would leave her and return to his brothers as if she were just another person in his life. That had always hurt Clare, because she wanted so much for Francis to care for her the way she cared for him.

It was only toward the end of his life when Francis lay terribly ill at San Damiano that he told her what his partings from her had cost him at the beginning.

The night she left her parents to join the brothers in the little chapel of Our Lady of the Angels, Francis had prayed and wept all night long, thanking the Father for this precious gift of Clare, thanking Jesus that his passion, death and resurrection had made their life together possible, and thanking the Holy Spirit who had come to Clare so powerfully that she too was now in love with God. Francis knew then that she understood how his love of God could take his heart from her, for her own love of God was now drawing her from him to God. Yet both of them through this common love were being drawn closer to each other than they were before.

How wonderful it all was in retrospect! And Clare also realized now that when she embraced the Lord with her vows of consecration, she had no longer needed to observe Francis to discern the will of God. God then spoke to her in the deep core of her own heart; and though she still turned to Francis for inspiration and light, her own faith was not dependent on him. The Lord had called her by name, and it was he who gave her the perfect gift of faith as before he had given her Francis' example and teaching. She was dependent on God, she was grateful for Francis, she loved them both.

*Once the realization is accepted that even be-
tween the closest human beings infinite distances
continue to exist, a wonderful living side by side
can grow up, if they succeed in loving the distance between them which makes it possible for
each to see the other whole against the sky.*

Rainer Maria Rilke

Brother Sun and Sister Moon

hy was the moon always visible when the sun was shining in Assisi? Even at midday when the sun was at its zenith, you could see the moon as well.* "Brother Sun and Sister Moon," Francis had called them. Could he have seen in these two heavenly bodies an image of himself and her? The sun, like the Father's love shining through Francis, lit up the moon which was Clare. The moon, the eternal symbol of woman. The moon which hangs

---

*Tourists remark that the sun and the moon appear together in the sky over Assisi with much greater frequency than they have noticed elsewhere.

in heaven shining and precious and fair. The moon whose reflection softens the garish radiance of the sun. The sun and the moon complemented each other and belonged together, and in Assisi they hung together in a cloudless sky every day.

This observation confirmed for Clare the rightness of their inseparable partnership in God's Kingdom. And she smiled to think that even a man who took seriously Christ's words about being a light to the world needed a moon to soften and complement God's radiance shining through him. She knew that Francis, too, had realized as much when he sang in ecstasy: "All praise be yours, my Lord, through Sister Moon and Stars; in the heavens you have hung them, bright and precious and fair."

Someone to Love

C lare made things for Francis. One winter when Francis was gone so long from Assisi, she embroidered an alb that took months to finish. Clare prolonged the work as long as possible because Francis and the brothers seemed so near while she sewed.

She always sat by the window when she was embroidering. Many times that winter when she looked up from her work, she thought she saw Francis coming down the road. But he never came, and her heart grew heavy worrying about him. She knew he was overtaxing himself, that in his love for his crucified Lord he never counted the cost to himself in bearing witness. How she longed to comfort him and do those little things a man appreciates so much from woman's hands and heart: to cook his meals, to wash his clothes, to press a cool damp cloth to his wearied brow. These she knew she could never do for him, and so she made things.

After he had been imprinted with the wounds of his crucified Lord, she made sandals and gloves for him. She had a hut built in the garden of San Damiano where she nursed him for 50 days when he was sick to the point of death. Those days were the fulfillment of all her years of longing to care for him, to minister to him who was her father in the Spirit.

Time meant nothing to Clare when she was doing something for Francis. No matter how pressing her duties as abbess became or how tired she was, she could start making something for Francis, and she would begin to relax, to experience inexplicable peace and rest in the Lord.

A Fruitful Barrenness

During the great high holy days Clare would think about Francis and celebrate in spirit with him. Christmas, especially, was dear to her because she knew how much that feast meant to Francis. She would see the child Jesus lying in the animals' feeding trough and thank the Father for this poor Christ whom she and Francis had seen being born anew in their own time. In some way, mysterious but real, she and Francis were there in the nativity scene beside the child, their virginal love so like that of Mary and Joseph that they too gave birth to him, and offered him to the world.

That thought made her barrenness fruitful and her virginity precious and warm and soft as a lover's touch. The delicate skin beneath her rough habit would seem fragrant with a sweet perfume, and Clare would feel so beautiful and so loved, and she would remember joyfully that she was a woman.

She no longer had that gnawing homesickness for Francis' presence that had haunted her in earlier days. She had learned to live apart, united only in mind and heart with him she loved. Clare had grown out of being in love and into loving. When that actually happened she couldn't remember, but she always celebrated this new love, this new level of loving, on the great high holy days of the Church.

Freedom from Boredom

When she looked at women her own age living comfortably and securely in

Assisi, Clare realized that Francis had saved her from boredom. How that was it was hard to explain. She was, after all, enclosed behind cloister walls, and anyone looking at her life, its routine, its "drabness," would surely have thought her mad to say her life was free from boredom.

But everything she was and everything she did was part of the great adventure God had revealed to Francis. The world was being reborn through the preaching and example of the friars and the prayer and poverty of the Poor Ladies of San Damiano. And so everything she did in that poor convent was charged with meaning, and meaning saves one from boredom and even from despair. What a small corner of the world was San Damiano! But from that place, as from the battlements of the most important castle, a message was going forth to the whole world, a message that every person on earth is blessed because Jesus Christ is Lord.

Clare needed only to observe her own companions to see the effect of a life lived wholly for the Lord. There was a radiant joy upon their faces, and they went about doing the humblest of tasks as if they were members of the papal court. The people of Assisi, too, proclaimed the beauty and significance of their lives. They came in steady lines to ask the Ladies' prayers and to have Clare lay her hands upon their sick. The Poor Ladies were never so much a part of the world as when they withdrew from it to dedicate their lives to God.

Even Francis, their father, turned to them for the support he needed in his ministry. Every success the friars had in building up the Kingdom of God was inspirited by the prayer of Clare and her Ladies. They were involved in a movement that stretched beyond San Damiano, beyond Assisi, even beyond Italy itself.

Leaving Home

her parents. How they suffered when she ran away from home! How Francis had suffered because they did not understand, because they believed he had seduced her into following the dream of a madman. Her father, especially, hated Francis, the wild son of Bernardone who had robbed him of his favorite daughter. He was jealous, too, because he knew Clare shared with Francis her inmost thoughts, those delicate, intimate confidences he felt she should have shared with him.

Clare suffered for all of them, for her parents and Francis and all the others she had to hurt in following the call of her Savior, Jesus Christ. Hurt! There was always hurt, it seemed, from beginning to end. Eventually there had come a sort of truce—at least grudging acceptance of what she had done. The pain became less severe, a sort of dull ache one grew used to and learned to ignore if there were to be any peace at all.

Francis had suffered so much misunderstanding in his own life that she winced to think she added to his burden. But it was Francis himself who encouraged her. He made it possible for her to stand against opposition in her response to Christ. When her father came with his knights to drag her forcibly back home, Clare thought she would die from the pain she saw in her father's eyes. It was the same disbelieving, wounded look she had imagined in Pietro Bernardone's eyes that day when Francis renounced his father before the bishop and the assembled citizens of Assisi.

She knew she would not succumb, not return with her father and his entourage, but it cut her deeply to cause him so much pain and grief, especially in front of his knights. How many sleepless nights she had spent in prayer for his forgiveness; how many times she wondered why following Jesus had to be so hard, so full of separation and alienation from those you loved.

And it was only when Ortolana, her widowed mother, came to live as a nun at San Damiano that Clare knew some peace over the pain she had caused. *Some* peace, because she never knew whether her father had forgiven her before he died. Her questioning of her mother about this was always met with vagueness and evasion, and Clare continued to weep for him. The desire for reconciliation was so deep that she longed for heaven where she would finally be able to tell it all to her wounded father and hear him say he understood.

This, too, she shared with Francis. Though he never told her, she knew he mourned his father's pain more than he ever showed. He would walk past his father's house, his eyes filled with tears as he looked up at the fastened shutters behind which the old man sat and brooded and railed his pain to Lady Pica.

Clare and Francis were orphans of sorts, fatherless children crying in the night for attention and love. They were comforted only by a heavenly Father who had called them to himself and who understood better than they that no one ever fully leaves father or mother, even for him. One only separates in time and place; the bond remains forever, whether you admit it or not.

Loneliness

I s there a cure for loneliness? Can the longing of the human heart be assuaged? Only in God, thought Clare, only in God. But how? Was it in loving him alone and closing your heart to others, avoiding risks, cautiously protecting yourself from involvement of any kind? How sterile that seemed, how dangerous—for the risk of not loving is greater than the risk of loving. Clare always refused to believe that the love of God meant withdrawal into oneself. On the contrary, it made possible a new love for others which left no room for loneliness, no time for self-pity.

Loving was always complicated, but *not* loving was even worse—impossible for her. She knew that love was her vocation, a love that embraced everyone and excluded no one. Her life at San Damiano, though relatively hidden and removed, was consciously motivated by her love of God and people. Everything that happened in Assisi was of interest to her because she was intimately involved in the lives of all its citizens, their troubles and their illnesses, their celebrations and their tragedies.

The cure for loneliness was a centering on the God who makes loving possible, then a reaching out to others in self-forgetfulness. Reaching out was beautiful and fragrant like the sweet scent of ginestra on the morning air. That is what it meant to Clare to say that only in God is there a balm for loneliness.

However, it was never just God up there in the heavens nor God in the depths of your own heart who healed you of loneliness. It was also God in the other: God in the poor, in the leper, in the lonely, in the sick and brokenhearted. Clare tried to teach the Poor Ladies this simple truth lest they withdraw into the luxury of thinking about themselves and God and the terrible selfishness of taking responsibility for no one.

Reaching out meant being responsible for others. If you were a contemplative, your love reached out to the whole world, and you took all the world's pain and suffering and confusion into your prayer and your loving. You were a part of everyone and everything, and you felt in a real way your connectedness with all of creation. Who could be lonely with so many to love, so many to care for, so many needs to present to the Father? That loving was complicated at times only assured Clare that she was still human, that she was loving as a woman instead of some sexless being trying to escape from the responsibility of being involved with mankind.

Loneliness was for the uninvolved, the self-seekers — unless you were in love with God, as Clare was. Then loneliness was really longing, a yearning to be with your beloved. That kind of loneliness would always be with her; it would always be her friend. But the loneliness which was self-preoccupation and self-pampering would always be a stranger in her house.

Longing drew you out; lonely self-pity drove you inwards. So there was a cure for loneliness, even though the longing of the human heart for God could not be completely satisfied here on earth.

> *God had called her through Francis to the literal following of Christ in the way of the Holy Gospel, and that call was absolute. It bound her to Francis in a union so close and so intimate that she saw it under the imagery of a child fed from its mother's breast.*
>
> *Lothar Hardick, O.F.M.*

A Vision

Clare dreamed often of Francis, but no dream moved her more than one that was more like a vision than a dream. She saw a high stairway, and she was climbing it as lightly as if she were on level ground. She was carrying a jug of hot water and a linen towel to Francis. When she finally reached him, he bared his chest and said gently, "Come and drink, my virgin, Lady Clare." And in the dream she drank something so sweet and delightful that she could not find words to describe it. When she drew away from him, a golden nipple remained between her lips. She took it reverently into her hand, and she saw in it her own reflection, as in a mirror. *

Over and over again she meditated on the vision and pondered its meaning. Was her relationship with Francis like that of a child fed at its mother's breast? Was he the incarnation of Jesus for her, the mediator of Jesus' own living water? Was she drinking of Francis' own spirit? Was his heart the mirror of her own? Or was it all of these dimensions together or separately, as she needed?

Whatever the meaning, that vision bound her to Francis anew and made him more present and tangible than if he were bodily before her. That the vision was from God she had no doubt. She received it and treasured it as a precious gift from her Father who understood how important Francis was to her and how intimately her life was bound to his.

Clare told no one of this vision except Sister Philippa, who of all her sisters would understand. Philippa said the vision was sacramental; Francis was the sacrament of the Lord for her. And Clare believed it was true.

---

*This vision is recorded in the process of Clare's canonization. *Cf.* Nesta de Robeck, *St. Clare of Assisi* (Milwaukee, Bruce, 1951), p. 197.

Letting Go

the only thing that kept her going at times was the fact that the Lord had brought her to San Damiano. It was not her doing, or fate, or some accident that she met Francis and fell under his spell. It was God's doing. So God would have to determine what it all meant and where it was supposed to lead; it was too much for her.

She wondered how those who didn't know the Lord survived separation from their loved ones or for that matter, how they survived any tragedy at all. And she was grateful once again for faith, for that gift that sustains the heart and gives meaning to the sometimes puzzle which is life.

Clare knew she had done nothing to deserve the faith she now had, and she felt an enormous sadness for those who were without it. As difficult as God seemed at times, at least she knew he existed and that he cared. Without him she could never persevere. It was difficult even to imagine life without faith in a living God who loved her and cared about her. And so she continued to put everything into his hands.

It was the letting-go that had been hardest to give to the Lord. Letting go of her parents, letting Francis move away, letting him be loved by others while she remained behind at San Damiano, letting him be. Yet she knew that was the only way—the denying, the love that doesn't cling, the heart made pure by giving away the beloved, the sharing. And once she did let go, Francis seemed closer to her than ever. It was always like that with the Lord. You struggled and wrestled with him for something and when you finally gave in and let go, he gave you freely what you had tried to wrest from him.

That was the way it had been in her struggle to hold on to Francis. She couldn't remember when or how she let go, but sometime at the beginning she had released him emotionally and given him back to the Lord. From that day on he was never far from her thoughts, and he was always in her heart. It was the Lord's doing, she was sure, and so she left the whole matter in his caring hands.

Since God had taken the initiative, she would let him continue to do so. And she would wait upon his will, she would receive only what and when God was ready to give. She, like his mother Mary, would wait and store up everything in her heart, trying to be his handmaid.

That would be the hardest test of all: to sit back and wait for God to effect what you would like to take into your own hands and accomplish through your own initiative. But Clare knew that really nothing could be accomplished by human effort alone; only the grace of God made anything possible. And so you learned to surrender to God, you learned to acknowledge your own helplessness, you learned that you could not control or be on top of everything in your life.

And once you learned that terrible lesson, everything made more sense. It was easier to let go, to trust, to believe that God would do more for you than you could do for yourself. First you had to wrestle with him, you had to try and beat him and go it alone and end up wounded. Then your surrender meant something. Then you felt that what God gave you as pure gift was something you had fought well to win on your own; you knew the worth of his gift and the impossibility of acquiring it by your own merits.

So Clare surrendered Francis to the Lord and waited for that moment when he would give him back—a moment which never came. For the Lord had been giving Francis to her all along and not in one dramatic moment.

The Lord had brought them together, and he had kept them together; yet they were separated from one another all their lives. What a paradox that was, how different from Clare's expectations in the beginning, from what she would have chosen for herself or wrested from God by force.

In the end she realized that what she really wanted was faith. She wanted to keep believing no matter what happened. She struggled with God for that precious gift, she was wounded in the battle, and she was weary and sick from fighting. And then one day she realized how strong her faith really was, that without her even realizing it, the Lord had already given her what she was still fighting for. In her struggle with God over Francis she had received the great gift of faith.

She believed God knew and understood and cared. She believed Francis and she were one in spirit though they were separated in body. Most of all she knew with the certainty of faith that Francis loved her and that in heaven they would know the fullness of each other's love and the fullness of their mutual sacrifice. And she let go and cried for joy and knew the worth of the Father's free gift.

In infinity already I see the dawn.
We shall be united forever in heaven.
Giuseppe Verdi

Death in October

Winters were hard at San Damiano. The lovely mists of summer that made the Valley of Spoleto blue against the mountains suddenly turned to wetness and damp, and Clare would feel a chill in every corner of her life. Sometimes the summer mists seemed to freeze in mid-air; just as her life would move from warm, liquid reverie to the sharp, pointed world of crystal. But always there was more sun than not, and Clare praised God for this reminder that summer would come again. Then she would let go and let winter purify her once more.

Clare's greatest letting-go came during that terrible winter of 1226. The winter she had dreaded for so many years began in early October. Though she knew Francis was dying, it all came so suddenly. One day he was alive; the next day the brothers were bringing his lifeless body to San Damiano and she was kneeling down before the bier looking on him whom she loved.

She saw in his hands and feet the marks of the
wounds of Christ and in his side the lance-wound as
well. She bent over and touched tenderly his
wounded side, and she burned with love for him who
now watched her from afar—or was he nearer than
he had ever been before? She kissed his hands and
feet and saw him smiling in eternity.

Clare suddenly felt an enormous sense of waste.
How much she could have given him during his life
had he let her, had they been different kinds of

people. But they weren't, and maybe that was the greatest reason Christ had kissed Francis with his own wounds.

Francis had deprived himself of all her womanly love and affection for so many years. Even during those 50 days he lay sick and feverish at San Damiano after descending the mountain of La Verna, he was strong in his resolve to hold her at a distance. She applied lotions to his eyes, but she did not kiss them; and her heart was sick that he should suffer so much alone without her consoling embrace.

How great Francis' love of God must have been to see in even the smallest intimacy with her a kind of coveting of his Lord's virgin bride. His life had been a constant letting-go, so now Clare in turn would let him go, as she had done so many times before. She knew it would be hard and that winter was threatening the valley where she lived. She could not think of that; it was too dark and cold a thought. Instead she looked up at Brother Sun and let Francis go and surrendered, for she knew that she would rise again, even from this . . . even from this.

Waiting for Eternity

h e was gone. Only memories now, open wounds flinching with every thought of him who had been so much a part of all she was and all she loved. Everything seemed to remind her of Francis: sudden birdsong from some distant cypress tree, a shaft of sunlight across her cheek, a man's voice on the road outside, a friar walking in the distance. She didn't cry much; she only hurt deep within.

From that day on there was less sunlight for Clare, and the song of the birds seemed melancholy, and the sky was grayer than she had ever remembered before. She was sick more, and her heart began to wait for that union with Francis in paradise. Whenever she was afraid she was forgetting, she would walk down to the chapel he had restored, touch the walls gently and kiss tenderly the cold, smooth stone—and he would be there. For the next 27 years not one day went by that Francis was not with her in prayer.

To others Clare seemed the same. She was always cheerful and giving, ever solicitous for the needs of all the Poor Ladies. But she had turned a lonely corner in her life, and there was darkness inside until she would walk once more with Francis. She knew their lives were so inextricably intertwined that they would be united again in heaven. And only then would be revealed the love they really had for one another.

She longed for heaven. She longed to be with Jesus and with her Francis. *Her* Francis! Now she could say that and not feel possessive or divided in her love. And she knew now that she was his Clare, he who never called anything his own.

Heaven was for those who had given everything and everyone away. Heaven was theirs, and heaven gave back what they had given away. In heaven *my* was a good and holy word again, especially for those who couldn't say it here on earth. Clare took comfort from that thought; and even though the sky turned gray and the sunlight seemed dimmer and the birds sang sadly, she would lift her heavy heart to the heavens and cry inside, "My Lord Jesus, I'm coming to you. I love you. My Francis, lead me again to your Lord."

A Lesson in Love

Francesco, the Frenchman. All his ways had been graced with the courtesy of the troubadours she had seen in her father's house, those French minstrels who knew so much of the science of lovemaking and so little of the art of love.

Clare smiled now as she remembered the songs of love she took so much to heart as a young girl. They had, in fact, been her dowry of mind and heart until she heard Francis talk of a love that outlasted the song and the melody. From the troubadours she had heard over and over again the formulas of love, the science of making a woman happy. Yet it was Francis who had made her supremely happy. And there was in him not even the shadow of idolatry of her, no trace or hint of infidelity to the Christ he loved above her, above all else that existed. The love of God, he said, transcends all we know of earthly love and yet embraces earthly love and sublimates it into an eternal human love. The meaning of his words, she, who loved him so, had learned through years of deprivation and sacrifice.

Now that he was in heaven, Francis was more present to her and more human than he had been when he walked the streets of Assisi. About human love Clare was sure she had known more than Francis had. But of divine love he was the master, and in the end that love had made him more human than she dared to believe he could become.

That was the mystery of it all, really, the divine becoming human. It started with Jesus, and Francis made it real again for her and for all his brothers and sisters. How much her Poor Ladies needed to know that very simple truth: If they would become human, they must become divine! Understanding that correctly, without heresy and without the subtle distinctions of the theologians, was her secret from Francis, her gift from her Seraphic Father who had loved God so intensely and perfectly that he ended up loving her. Only one who loves God above all can love a woman as she should be loved, selflessly, totally, with God's own love enfleshed in a poor little man.

A Mountain Man

*n*ot everyone was safe out there on the mountain as Francis had been, for he was a mountain man and understood its moods. He had known how to make the mountain his friend. The mountain helped to keep away the world and its distractions, to restore his broken spirit when he had been too long on the road, to hide him from those who were taxing his patience and his strength.

For years Clare meditated with her eyes fixed on Mount Subasio. She would imagine she saw Francis up there surrounded by ginestra, lying on his back with his hands behind his head. He would be watching the swallows soaring in the sky high above. There would be larks and smaller birds flitting from bush to bush because they could not fly as high, and Francis would notice them too. He was a mountain man; he knew how to see what was around him.

In their long talks together before she joined the brothers at the Portiuncula, Francis had shared with her his love of the mountain. He told her how he loved the storms up there and the fresh odor the olive trees gave off after a short rain when the clouds blew over and the sun came out again. He told how he was never afraid up there because he and the mountain were friends and how one day he would sing its praises when he was old enough to sing them well.

He never sang the mountain song for her; he died before he knew enough to sing it. But he sang that

other song of Brother Sun, and it contained
something of what the earth had told him, perhaps
everything the earth had told him. Clare knew that
most of what he sang about nature he had learned on
Mount Subasio. And this is what he sang, this is how
he said it:

Praised be You, my Lord, through all Your
    creatures,
Especially Sir Brother Sun,
Who makes the day and enlightens us
    through You,
He is lovely and radiant and grand;
And he heralds You, his Most High Lord.

Praised be You, my Lord, through Sister
    Moon
And through the stars.
You have hung them in heaven shining and
    precious
And fair.

And praise to You, my Lord, through
    Brother Wind,
Through air and cloud, calm and every
    weather
That sustains your creatures.

Praised be You, my Lord, through Sister
    Water,
So very useful, humble, precious and chaste.

Yes, and praise to You, my Lord, through
    Brother Fire.
Through him You illumine our night,

And he is handsome and merry, robust and
   strong.

Praised be You, my Lord, through our
   Sister, Mother Earth
Who nourishes us and teaches us,
Bringing forth all kinds of fruits and colored
   flowers
And herbs.

It was all there between the lines; so much was said
between the lines with Francis! He had always called
her Lady Clare, and that said more than most people
realized. He sang of a sun that was masculine and a
moon that was feminine, and of wind and fire that
were a different sex from water and earth; that too
said more than even she dared to guess. What goes
on in the deep heart of a poet who praises God
through creatures, none of whom are plant or
animal, and all of whom rest between a masculine
sun and a feminine earth?
   Clare was a woman of the plain, but she too had
traveled the mountain, that other mountain of the
inner mind where the elements of the world become
the geography of your own soul. You make them
your own and praise God through them, for they
have become the stuff of your own self, of who you
are. You praise God through earth and water and air
and fire because that is what you are made of; and if
you are a poet like Francis, you know how to pair
them and how to describe them and what value they
have.
   Francis had indeed been a mountain man, but he

was a poet and mystic too. She who knew him so well understood why he saw her face in the moon and called it precious and fair. That is why he sang his poem first of all for her; she was Clare, a light, his light, and she heard his voice between the lines of his poetry and his life. She was the moon only a mountain man could see. *

Memories

She realized she was no longer young. She lived each day to the full and tried to be wholly present to her prayer and her work, but more and more she noticed herself slipping imperceptibly into memory. And her memories seemed always good. She would remember the glorious days of her youth as she listened to Francis preach, the long honeymoon of those first years at San Damiano and the lovely times when Francis and the brothers would come to share what God had done for them upon the road. It all became lovelier in memory.

This is what it was to be older: You had the memories of ecstasies that the young thought only

---

*This meditation relies upon the ideas of Father Eloi Leclerc, O.F.M., developed so profoundly in his book, *The Canticle of Creatures: Symbols of Union* (Chicago, Franciscan Herald Press, 1977).

they understood. You, too, had been loved. You, too, had loved and felt the warmth run through all your body; you had run through the poppy fields outside the walls of Assisi and shouted your joy to the sky. You, too, had believed it all would last forever. Then somewhere in between youth and now you lost it, that vision, that radiant dream of youth— only to rediscover it more tranquilly and more completely in memory's mansion, that peaceful refuge of the aging lover.

Imagination, too, played a part; for Clare felt nothing could really have been so beautiful as the beginning of their dream now seemed from the vantage point of a woman 58 years old. As soon as she thought of 58, she felt strangely young again, for what were so few years, after all, to one who never tired of singing God's praises? At that moment she wanted many more years if only to share the memory of Francis' ideal with hundreds of women to come. The memory would keep alive the dream of what life could be if one surrendered wholly to the Lord and shared that life with others. Old age gave hope and wisdom to the young when the memories were as precious and pure as Clare's.

She grew up of very great beauty and when she was 12 they wished to marry her; but she obtained a delay which she used to prepare quite other projects of her own.

Omer Englebert

A Love Story

C lare had always loved the Feast of San Rufino, the patron saint of Assisi. It reminded her of her childhood home next to the church of San Rufino. The feast would bring back to mind the ringing of the bells late into the night and the torches burning gaily in the bell tower and in the piazza of San Rufino. It was a time for dressing in all your finery and attending the High Mass with the Bishop of Assisi presiding. She remembered seeing Francis there as a young man, always impeccably dressed, always outshining everyone else in the cut and quality of his clothes.

The first time she noticed him she was six years old, and she made up her mind then and there that she would marry him as soon as possible. Her mother assured her that could never be. First of all, Francis was not noble; secondly, her father had someone else in mind; and finally, she only had a bad case of "puppy love."

And then Alberto!* How he had suffered when she ran away to join Francis at the Portiuncula. That was the hard side of love, especially the kind of love she had chosen: Someone was always left out, someone who loved you deeply as a man loves a woman, someone who also had dreams—dreams of sharing his life with you and sleeping with you beneath the Umbrian sky. Alberto had loved her so much and then hated her for awhile, only to love her again, finally resigning himself to his fate. He was a knight and a very famous singer of poems, and Clare was sure his relationship with her over the years had inspired his greatest poems. She had saved a packet of letters which he had never sent her but which were given to her when Alberto died. Now as the bells again rang in the Feast of San Rufino and she remembered her childhood and early teens, she opened them to read reverently another love story.

I

How long now, Clare, since I first saw you standing shyly behind your mother, watching the water sparkle in the morning sun? You held your mother's hand and your eyes stood transfixed before the spouting water of the fountain in the Piazza del Comune. My heart took flight and broke out of the dark forest of my fears and doubts. Little did I know then

---

*When a girl as young and beautiful as Clare consecrates herself to the Lord, there is often someone left behind. Alberto is a symbol of all those who feel rejected when someone they love "leaves them" for a life dedicated to God. He is based upon a real person, a knight to whom Clare was promised when she was about 16, but whom she refused to marry. *(Cf.* Heribert Roggen, *The Spirit of St. Clare* [Chicago, Franciscan Herald Press, 1971], p. ix.)

what pain you would cause me, what frustration. Little could I have known then that I was not a part of God's plan for you. I say that almost without bitterness now. I even speak of God again: God, my terrible rival; God, who took you from me; God, who proved too strong, too invisible for me to fight. Well you're his now. Let him take you! And when I see your silhouette behind the grille at San Damiano, I pray he's been good to you, though that dark, private cloister makes me fear he is more jealous than I would have been.

But that is all behind us, isn't it? Why do I even have to write these banal confessions? So, as the troubadours say, *voila.* Yes, *voila.* But you cannot hear my tone of voice, can you? *Voila,* Clare, *viola.* There is still an edge to my voice. God grant that these random scratchings of a failed poet might take that edge away forever.

Does it hurt you to hear me calling myself a failed poet? I know you blame yourself as I once did, but there is more to failure than that, my Clare. Yes, you are still *my* Clare when I am not careful. "My Clare" slipped out the other day when I was talking to one of the little brothers. Do you know what that feels like? How *could* you in your careful cloister with silence sealing your heart? But as I was saying, there is more to failure than losing you. In fact, Clare, had you not left me, I would not have written at all. Now, at least, one poem is good: the poem of your leaving.

96

How strange! Even that last statement came out with an edge on it. But, as I said, I am not bitter. I am trying to understand. Perhaps that is too much to ask, but I must try. I can no longer bear to wake suddenly to the curious stares of people and hear their snickers and the snide little, "He is a crazy middle-aged poet. No one knows why he suddenly cries out, 'Clare!' She must have been his mistress. Maybe his Muse. Maybe both." And then they laugh and turn to their affairs. And some pain me even more by the pity in their eyes.

I don't need pity. I just need to understand. I just need to stop thinking, but I can't. So now I think on paper. And this, Clare, is what I think. This is our story.

Our story. Two words on paper and already I am almost honest. *Voila.* Honesty. Let it come. The flood.

You were 13 that day at the fountain. You were Clare of Favorone and Ortolana, and I was Alberto Humberti. I was 14, and I knew immediately that you were the one. I was alone, as usual, standing just inside a portico where I could watch you without your seeing me. How foolish I was to think you would have noticed me. That is the way with dreamers, *cara.* They foolishly think people see their thoughts in their eyes, that they will be found out.

I remember the white satin dress you wore that day and the gold brocade that looked like a sash about your slender waist. Your pointed red slippers made your feet seem so fragile and small. I wondered how they bore your weight, and I imagined you skimming above the surface of the earth like an otherworldly being. Now that I am older and you have been a nun so long, I still see you as the little girl with the white satin dress standing by your mother in the Piazza del Comune.

Someone told me once that I would forget the loves of my youth, and I wanted to believe him. I tried to believe him. How futile that effort was! For 30 years I thought I had erased your memory only to wake up in old age with your image alive and well in my mind. I am done with forgetting, so I try now to remember the way it never was with us; I remember the way I would like for it to have been . . .

I am not old, really; only the years away from you make it seem that way.

II

It is hard for me to contain my bitterness, Clare, because what I longed for and dreamed of, Francis got: your love and unflagging devotion. I never wanted more than he wanted, Clare; perhaps to hold you, but nothing more. I only wanted to be loved. And I wanted you to be the one who loved me. How strange love is. It comes to those who are not necessarily looking for it and sometimes even to those who are trying to avoid it, like your Francis. And those who seek it and yearn for it end up writing about it from frustration and a need for someone to know that they, too, are human, that they, too, matter in the drama where only the main actors are remembered.

I love you, Clare, even though now you are

really more imaginary to me than real; it has been so long a time since I saw you. You are my inspiration and my reason for living, and I have never even spent an hour alone with you. How strange love is. Perhaps I am not a worthless poet. Perhaps my love for you is the only thing that is clean and beautiful in my life. I never even thought of that until I wrote that sentence. I never realized that maybe I am as good as you are, that maybe I am as constant as Francis is, that in my own way I count for something just because I have never stopped loving even though the love I wanted never responded to me, never noticed me, in fact. So you see, Clare, you have helped me love myself. By never experiencing even the smallest return for my love, I have learned to love you for yourself and not for what you might do for me. And even these lines which I wanted so much to send you, you will never read. Only in heaven, my Clare, will you know that you have been loved as much as you loved Francis. I only pray that because of you I will be there in heaven, too, and you will turn your head and look at me and love me for never saying anything on earth, for never disturbing your perfect peace, for not being selfish. Dear God, help me to be there and don't let eternity be what time has been for me.

III

O, Clare, how often I dreamed of praying with you, my saint, of kneeling beside you and sharing a place before God with you. Perhaps I still sell myself short, Clare, but I cannot image a man like me coming alone before God. With you I would not be afraid. And so, Clare, when I pray alone in my room or in the church of San Rufino, I imagine you are there beside me; and God hears me because you are there. I pray this way, Clare, not because I do not think God loves me, but because I love you and cannot do anything without you, and because I know you are holy, Clare, someone special to God. At the beginning I couldn't stand that fact and constantly resented a God who had the whole universe and insisted on taking you from me who had nothing and wanted only you. It was like one of the lords who insists on some poor peasant's wife when he could choose from all the beauties in the land. Then one day I realized that you loved him and that he never forced you to love him.

With Francis it was different for me. I never felt he gave you half of what you deserved, my Clare. He is so wrapped up in God and in his way of life, that even you, Clare, are a threat to his Dream. He knows you love him, but he won't let you touch him. He only uses you to further his own movement of Evangelical Poverty, Chastity and Obedience. Perhaps that is too harsh, but that is the way I see it, and I, of course, am jealous.

O Clare, why must I always think of Francis when I think of you? If he had not whisked you away so young, before I had time to come to you, had not stolen your heart before I was ready to let you go, of all men on earth, I would consider him most blessed and most perfect. And perhaps I consider him such even now after so much grief and so much pain. How subtly he works even on me. How can I blame you for running after him?

IV

Clare, sometimes in the night, when the wind beats against my window and drives drops of rain into my heart, I think of you at San Damiano and how cold it must be there inside the austere dwelling you have made for yourself and your companions. And I cannot understand why. I try, but reason and imagination, my gifts, fail me whenever I think of you. I know that you, unlike me, are warm inside with God's love, but why all this penance, this pain you inflict upon yourself? It hurts me, Clare, more than you, I know. And when I think of Francis on Mount Subasio sleeping in his cave, colder and more austere yet, my confusion grows. You two, so removed, so remote from one another are so much closer than the lovers I watch at evening time walking hand in hand in the Piazza del Comune. How weak my mind becomes; how insufficient even poetry is to explain this.

V

Clare, I think I understand the way it is with you, how you can be so happy with so little in this life and with so frustrated a love as you have had with Francis. It is simple, really, something I should have seen from the beginning: If you have nothing and expect nothing, then everything that comes is a gift, an unexpected joy. I have seen so many, Clare, who had everything anyone could reasonably expect from life, including love; and yet they are not as happy as you.

VI

Now your Francis is all alone, Clare. You knew it would come to this, as I did. Always, like his Christ, the saint finds himself alone in his own Gethsemane. You have not left Francis, of course, but he has left you and everyone else because he has to act out this scene alone. None of us is spared this kind of suffering, this terrible aloneness, which I'm sure even you, Clare, have felt often as you sat alone in your cell and wondered where your God had fled to and who it was who really led you to this place, this time of life.

You know Francis will come back stronger, don't you? You know that when he comes down from La Verna, he will be so totally God's that he will be yours forever. There will be some purification upon that mountain that will seal forever the bond of love between you. My own suffering for you will never do that for us, because it is you I want, not God. And besides, my own aloneness is over now, Clare. There are others in my life and you become more and more like a dream I wake to now and then, not the obsession you were so many years ago.

VII

Clare, I remember you in the early dawn skipping across the Piazza del Comune to San Georgio's and myself dreaming of the day we would stand at the altar in that little church and vow our love forever. Always it was the same, my fantasies outreaching common sense. I hardly knew you and yet you were always on my mind. You were someone I would win, someone who would be mine, though I didn't even have a plan. In my youthful naivete, I somehow presumed you would one day notice me, and you would know everything once you looked into my eyes.

I don't see that as foolish, Clare, even now so many years after my adolescent dreams, because I know that when you *did* look at me, *did* see me watching you at parties or in the piazzas of Assisi, you knew. You knew, I'm sure, in the way you shyly looked away. But always you looked away slowly, carefully as if afraid you would hurt me, or that something inside me would fall and break if you glanced away too quickly. Your dreams were so different from mine, Clare; yet isn't it strange that those dreams have come together like some strange alchemy in the lines I write to you who will never read them? Perhaps we're closer than you and Francis ever were, for no one knows our hearts and what we really think and feel the way they know Francis. We are the silent partners in God's plan for Francis, the ones who stand in shadows and support him unawares.

It never struck me before, actually, that I supported him, but I have in all the prayers I've said that he would lead you safely to that dream you had of being poor like him and living only for the Lord. And now he's dead, and you are alone with God and with other women whose pettiness weighs you down and makes you wonder what will happen when you die. Do you wonder about that, my Clare? You need not. Even I can see your dream will outlive both you and your Francis. There is something magical in the two of you, you know, something otherworldly, divinely inspired, like one or two poems I know will outlive the passing fame I now enjoy.

But what was I going to say when all these memories crowded in again? No matter now, for all is memory anyway or fantasy that hasn't quit for 30 years. My lady, what power you possess to hold me bound this way. How sweet the binding, that I should never have tried to free myself.

VIII

I keep returning to Assisi, as to some shrine or place of pilgrimage, and I walk back and forth beside the convent where you live; I don't know what I'm looking for or what I expect to find in these frequent visits to this place of pain and sorrow. Perhaps it is for me, as for so many others, unbearable to face the end of something beautiful, be it only in the mind. And so I return perversely to keep the fantasy of you alive. It's not that you haunt me or disturb me anymore. It is just my own tenacious love that will not let go because of all the years gone by, all the time already spent in hanging on to the dream you've finally become for me.

You no longer matter, Clare, because the dream of you is now more real than you who live behind these cloister walls. I've not seen the real you for so long, I wonder if I'd know you, were you suddenly to look out a window and wave to me. You've changed, no doubt, as I have. No matter, really. The young girl who walked into this convent long ago leaped into my mind and lives there young and fresh, more beautiful today for all the love I've spent in keeping her alive.

You must think me mad, Clare, to talk this way about a dream that seems merely to fire a fevered brain. Perhaps I am, but madness such as this makes all my ways a light and airy dream. I shall return again next year, and you will still be there inside those walls because you'll live inside my dream, a dream nourished more by the walls through which you disappeared than by the face I never see behind them.

IX
O, Clare, how you haunt my days and ways

away from you. Each time I return like this I feel your presence and I quicken my pace up this winding road to Assisi. I am afraid, I guess, that you'll not be here this time, that God will snatch you away before he takes me from this earth. Why do I cling to you this way? So many years and still you draw me with an irresistible pull of the heart. Sometimes I think it must be me and not you who keeps this thing alive. It is you, of course, but a you I knew so long ago that I think I must be insane to be in love with a memory, a brief encounter; not even that really, but a wish, a dream of you I fashioned out of pen and ink and what I wanted you to be.

I've left you time and time again, and told myself how crazy I was to keep this dream alive. But somehow, after so many years in madness, I've grown accustomed to this fantasy I live by. Perhaps that is how your God is with you, Clare, a dream of what you hoped he'd be. I know that must sound like blasphemy to you. I'm sorry; my thoughts grow more foolish with the passing years. I'm really not so bad as you might think. Why, just the other day I started praying once again. I knew you'd like that, Clare.

And she lifted her eyes toward Assisi and the joyous bells of San Rufino, and she prayed a tender prayer for Alberto. He, too, was a part of her story, for she had carried him in her heart and prayed for him from the moment she had walked away from his young and wounded life.

He visited Clare and she more often him, so ar-
ranging the times of their visits that this divine
pursuit might not be known by man or objected
to by public gossip. Only a lone trusted compan-
ion accompanied the girl when she left her paren-
tal home to hold secret meetings with the man of
God . . . .

Thomas of Celano

Full Moon Over Assisi

It was full moon over Assisi and in her heart, and
the silver-green leaves of the olive trees below her
window reminded her of those nights so long ago
when she and Francis used to meet beneath the stars,
and he would fill her heart with Jesus. It seemed only
the night before that he had sat beside her. No one
ever knew of those meetings but Brother Philip and
Lady Bona, who were also present, and Sister Moon
and the bright and precious stars that shone upon
those sacred hours they shared together. Both of
them knew those times couldn't last forever, and so
they treasured each meeting as if it were their last.

Those nightly meetings beneath the Umbrian sky
forged the bond between them that was to last all
their lives. And now Francis was a saint in heaven,
solemnly proclaimed so by the Holy Father himself.
How strange that felt, especially on this moonlit
night when she saw Francis in her mind's eye as a
young man sitting by her side and looking into her

eyes with a terrible earnestness that would have been humorous in anyone else. And as he spoke of Jesus and his sufferings, his eyes would always begin to fill with tears.

The moon was in full view over Mount Subasio now, and Clare realized that there were tears in her eyes, too. She blinked them away and lifted her face to the moon. And there sailing across the moon was a little cloud the shape of a Tau cross, appearing to bless her upturned face. And Clare looked at the moon and saw her own face smiling down upon Assisi, and all the olive trees of Umbria turned from green to silver.

Clare strove by perfect poverty to be made like the Poor Crucified, that no passing thing of earth might separate the lover from the Beloved or hinder the course of her union with God.

Thomas of Celano

Dreams Are for Sharing

Dreams are for sharing. Sharing dissolves the loneliness of the dream's pursuit and clarifies its meaning. Her nature was brightness, was light, and perhaps that was why Francis had invited her to share the vision Christ had shown him. And she had kept the light of his dream shining through all the darkness of the years, a darkness that descended upon their lives soon after Francis' death.

The brothers had depended so heavily on Francis to keep their own dreams alive that when he died, the brotherhood was split into factions over the meaning of his dream of poverty. She knew what that poverty was, that it was something new and untried, that she and Francis and their followers had stood against all the conventional lifestyles of the Church and insisted on the practicality of their way of life. And the Pope himself had approved the poverty of Francis.

Why then was there so much disagreement over poverty and so much darkening of this new light that had dawned upon the world? Wasn't it because something else had died out? Poverty, after all, was not the light of the world, and it was not poverty that Francis loved above all else. Always it was Jesus Christ, his suffering Lord and Savior, who was the light. It was Jesus he loved and his poverty that Francis embraced.

Why couldn't the brothers see that it was Jesus who had died out in their hearts? They had unwittingly replaced him with an idea, the idea of poverty. How sad it is that when the love of the Lord dies out in the human heart, the mind replaces him with an idea to be lived, and how different that is from a person to be loved! Francis had loved and followed the poor Jesus. It was as simple as that, and no amount of arguing could tell you how to do that or define the limits of loving or being poor.

And so she fought to keep the light of love shining on the poor, crucified Christ. If they would only keep him before their eyes, the rest would follow.

But that is precisely what so many couldn't do. She wondered sometimes if Francis had in fact replaced Jesus in their minds. Dreams are for sharing, and the dream she and Francis had shared was the literal following of the Christ of the Gospels. They had had to follow him by the light of their own hearts and minds illumined by the Spirit and his Church. The brothers would have to do the same. Arguing was not sharing the dream, nor would disputes over poverty ever illumine the darkness left when the love of Christ dies out in the human heart.

The Privilege of Poverty

Unbarring the locked door and sneaking out at night and stealing down to the Portiuncula in the moonlight, the wind nervously shaking the tiny olive leaves. The brothers waiting on the road with torches in their hands, their faces flushed by the flames, and Francis clipping her hair and the yellow locks falling lifeless onto the dirt floor. The disappointment and pain of having no home and then Francis bringing her to San Damiano and the joy of the Poor Ladies there in that precious little church that Francis himself had restored and their happy life there where everything was poor. Her battle with the Pope for the privilege of living in complete poverty and now his giving in and the announcement that he was this day to

111

secure for her and the Poor Ladies the privilege of poverty forever . . .

Toward the end it all got mixed up in her mind.

It had taken over 40 years for that to happen. But now as she lay in bed with the scent of death in the air, it all danced at once in her mind and her whole life was like a day, a moment of celebration.

Clare looked at the bare ceiling of the dormitory. Her eyes wandered wearily over the plain stone walls, and it all became a palace of poverty, a rich simplicity that she had spent her whole life preserving. She tried not to be possessive even of this impoverished place, for it was a place, after all, and her Lord and Savior Jesus Christ had no place to lay his head. Even from San Damiano she must be as detached as Francis was, for even the poorest place can become a rich possession for one who has nothing. Clinging to San Damiano was especially dangerous because of its association with Francis.

And then the little swallows who nested in the rafters of the ceiling began to fly in and out singing their excitement in the morning sun, and she remembered how Francis had always returned to the Portiuncula. It wasn't so much a place as a nest, a womb, a center where God had spoken, a source of renewal for the spirit. San Damiano was a sacred space where Lady Poverty lived. There you moved in her presence easily, warmed at the hearth of silence and renunciation, if God so willed. Clare would go wherever the Pope sent her, but wherever she went she would take Lady Poverty with her, and around her and the Poor Ladies would grow another holy space where the poor Christ would dwell.

She closed her eyes with effort, even that simple movement taxing her waning strength. She slept and the dreams kept rushing in. The dreams of memory.

Mercenary soldiers were in the courtyard again and she was shakily holding the ciborium in the open door. The quizzical looks on their faces and horses pawing the ground, their nervous neighs charging the tense atmosphere, and her prayers to the Eucharistic Christ and their panic and retreat as if from some invisible army. And fire filled the sky over the Portiuncula and she saw herself and Francis and the brothers eating a meal in the open. She was listening to Francis and speaking with him and the word Jesus *flew back and forth. It increased in speed and it caught fire and she and Francis were all light and the Seraphim beat the air with hot wings and the breath of God warmed the whole valley . . .*

She felt something at her wrist. She painfully lifted her eyelids and the room was on fire. At the foot of her straw mat stood one of the brothers, and in his hand he held the confirmation of her Rule of Life and the Privilege of Poverty from Innocent, the Vicar of Christ. She took it weakly in her open palm and its strength drove her hand to her heart and she slept.

The holy virgin turning to herself began to speak softly to her soul: "Go forth without fear, for you will have a good escort on your journey. Go forth," she said, "for He who created you has sanctified you. He has protected you always as a mother does her child, and has loved you with a tender love." Then she added, "Blessed be you, my Lord, who have created me!"

Thomas of Celano

Sister Death

Clare knew she was dying, and she couldn't believe how much like life it was. She had known physical and mental suffering for so many years that this new experience seemed like meeting an old, familiar friend. She welcomed Sister Death because she had no fear of her, because it was death who would bring her into life. It was Sister Death who would return Francis to her at last and bring before her eyes the Lord Jesus whom she had loved with all her heart and soul. This was not death, as other people knew death: an impersonal "it" bringing separation and pain. This was life; all those years of separation from Francis and her Lord were that impersonal death which others feared so much and tried so hard to postpone.

Her sisters were gathered around her now. And what was this? Here were Brothers Angelo, Leo and Juniper, her faithful friends. They had become even more dear to her after Francis' death, and she remembered now that she had sent for them to read the Passion of Jesus to her on her bed of pain. They had come to watch one hour with her.

Leo knelt and kissed the straw of her mat; Angelo consoled everyone, as usual; and Juniper began reading the Passion of the Lord in his inimitable, enthusiastic manner. Clare listened with great peace and joy, and then she said to all in the room, "Do you not see the King of Glory? Here he is before me."

She never knew if they saw the Lord or not, for she was caught up in the vision before her. Then the mother of Jesus entered the room and took Clare into her arms and carried her into heaven. And the light in the garden flamed high, the fire of its passing warming Assisi forever.

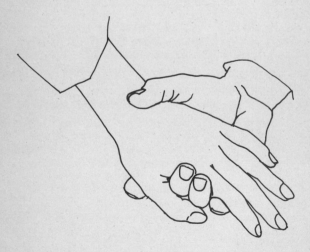

Appendix

Any chapter of this book taken singly would certainly be misleading as a portrait of St. Clare. Even the whole book is but a partial picture composed of snapshots taken from different angles; for no biography, no story can tell it all, can present that multi-dimensional picture which is a life. Some of what I have not said, I let Clare herself say in these letters which present a further dimension of who she is. The four letters*, composed roughly between 1234 and 1253 and addressed to Blessed Agnes of Prague are unquestionably authentic and give us a glimpse into the soul of Clare.

Agnes was the daughter of King Ottokar I of Bohemia and Queen Constance of Hungary. She had been promised in marriage to Henry VII of Germany, but Henry married Margaret of Austria instead. Henry III of England then sought her hand, but Agnes refused further suitors and dedicated herself to Christ. She heard of Francis and Clare from the missionary Friars who came to Prague. In 1232 and 1233 she built a church and friary and then a monastery attached to a hospital for the poor. Agnes herself entered this Monastery of the Most Holy Redeemer in 1234. There she desired to live with her companions the life Clare and her Poor Ladies lived at San Damiano. She died in 1282 and was beatified by Pope Pius IX in 1874.

LETTER I

1. To the venerable and most holy virgin, the Lady Agnes, the daughter of the most excellent and illustrious king of Bohemia, Clare the unworthy servant of Jesus Christ and the unworthy handmaid of the Cloistered Ladies of the Monastery of San Damiano, with special respect commends herself as one subject to all and set to serve all,

---

*Translation by David Temple, O.F.M.

and wishes you the prize of eternal happiness.

2. I have heard the most wonderful report of your truly holy manner of life and conduct. This word has come not only to me but is spread about generally all over the world. This gives me great joy in the Lord and I am lifted up by it. The strong current of this joyful response has carried not only this far but everywhere to hearten those who serve Jesus Christ or who desire to serve him. This has happened because you could have enjoyed pomp and honor and high place in this world beyond the reach of anyone else. It was yours, if you had so wished, with full right to marry the great Emperor, in circumstances that were in accord with his dignity and with yours. But you set aside all these things with full intent of heart and unswerving purpose of soul. You have chosen rather most holy poverty and spare support for bodily needs. You have united yourself to a Spouse of more noble lineage, the Lord Jesus Christ. He will guard your virginity spotless and untarnished. "Whom when you have loved, you are chaste; when you have touched, you are purer yet; whom when you have taken to yourself, you are a virgin." His power is greater than that of any other; his nobility is more exalted; his countenance is more beautiful; his love is sweeter; and his courtesy is more gracious. You are already held fast by his embrace. He has adorned your breast with precious stones and has provided priceless pearls for your ears. He has set you about wholly with jewels that shine with a brightness like the springtime. He has placed upon your head a golden crown as a symbol of holiness.

And so it is, dearest sister, or better I should say, dear lady worthy of great regard and respect, because you are the spouse and the mother and the sister of my Lord, you are signed in most brilliant fashion with the sign of inviolable virginity and most holy poverty. Stand firm in the service which you have undertaken! You have taken a strong position and you have made a courageous beginning in a desire to come to the poor Crucified who for our sake took upon himself the suffering of the cross and thus freed us from the power of the prince of darkness, in which we were held because of the fall of our first parent, and who made peace for us with God the Father.

3. O blessed poverty, which brings eternal riches to those who love it and embrace it! O holy poverty—to those who possess and desire you God promises the kingdom of heaven and without doubt eternal glory and a most happy and blessed life. O poverty dear to God, which our Lord Jesus Christ, who made heaven and earth and rules them all, who spoke the word and the world was made,—it was he who bent down to embrace proverty. He said the foxes have their dens and the birds of the air their nests, but the son of man—that is Christ himself—does not have whereupon to lay his head, but bowing his head he gave up his spirit.

It was God of such splendor and such greatness who entered the womb of the Virgin. It was his choice to be despised, needy and poor in this world so that men who were so very poor and in such deep need and in dire hunger of heavenly nourishment might be made rich in him and possess the heavenly kingdom. Therefore you should respond with full joy of spirit and set no limit to your rejoicing and you should be filled with a mighty joy and in true spiritual happiness because you have chosen to set aside the world rather than to be drawn in quest of its honors. You have large reasons to rejoice because it has been your choice to seek poverty in preference to riches which might be held by human hands in these times. Rather than lay up treasure on earth you have set your treasure in heaven where the rust does not consume it, nor the moth eat holes in it, nor thieves break in and steal it away. Because you have acted thus your reward will be very rich in heaven and you have with full right merited to be called the sister, spouse and mother of the Son of the Father Most High and of the glorious Virgin (Mt 6:20).

4. I believe very firmly that you know very well that the kingdom of heaven is promised by the Lord to only the

118

poor and to them it is given, because when the heart is set on some temporal thing the fruit of charity is lost. It is not possible to serve God and mammon, because you will either love the one and hate the other or you will serve the one and despise the other (Mt 6:24).

Fix your attention first on what has prime place in this mirror, and this is the poverty of the babe who is placed in the manger and wrapped in swaddling clothes. What tremendous humility we find here and what astounding poverty! The king of the angels and the lord of heaven and earth is resting in a manger. In the center of the mirror consider long and carefully the humility which walks side by side with blessed poverty, and the countless labors and hardships which he bore for the redemption of the human race. And, finally, in studying the last features of the mirror, open your mind and your soul to the unspeakable love which prompted him to want to suffer on the gibbet of the cross and there to die the most shameful kind of death. Let us give our full attention to what the same mirror, placed on the wood of the cross, sets before the eyes of all who pass by: "Oh all you who pass by the way, attend and see if there be any sorrow like my sorrow." Let me answer with one voice and one spirit him who calls out and laments: "I recall in my soul and my heart grows faint within me." (Lam 1:12 and 3:20). When you respond in this way each time you will be caught up more mightily in the fire of love, O queen of the heavenly King.

5. Take a long, loving look also at the delights which cannnot be described in words and which he brings to you, and the riches, and the honors that have no dateline to end them. Responding to the greatness of all this, with all the fullness of desire of which your heart is capable and all the love that it can summon, shout out in joy: "Draw me! After you we shall run in the odor of your ointments, heavenly bridegroom! I shall run, lest I faint, until you lead me in to the storeroom, until your left hand is under my head and until your right arm will happily embrace me, and until you will kiss me with the most

joyful kiss of your mouth." When you are so wrapt in contemplation, think of me, your little poor mother, and remember that I have the thought of you sculpted deeply on the tablets of my heart. There you are dearer than anyone else in the world.

6. What else shall I say? When I speak of my love for you the tongue of the flesh is locked up in silence; but the tongue of the spirit has a thousand words to say. O most blessed daughter, because the tongue of the flesh cannot possibly in any further manner express the love which I have for you, it is nonetheless setting down these things which are about half of what I wished to say. I beg you with all the deepest regard for you that you will at least be able to pick up out of them the deep feeling of a mother which I have for you and for your daughters.

This true love is with me every day. In Christ I do wish to commend to you most completely myself and my daughters. All of them and especially Agnes, that very prudent virgin and our sister, wish in whatever manner they possibly can to commend themselves in the Lord and to you and to your sisters.

7. Farewell, dearest daughter, and a farewell to your daughters, unto the throne of glory of the great God and pray for us! The Friars who bear this letter to you are very dear to us. Brother Amato, loved by God and men, and Brother Bonagura, in as much as I am able, I do by this present plea commend to your charity. Amen.

LETTER II

1. To the daughter of the King of Kings, to the handmaid of the Lord of lords, to the most worthy spouse of Jesus Christ and therefore the queen and the lady noble beyond compare Agnes, Clare the useless and unworthy handmaid of the Poor Ladies, wishes health and power and the will to live always in the highest poverty.

2. I give thanks to the giver of all grace from whom every best gift and every perfect benefit, as we believe, comes

forth (Jas 1:17). I wish to render him thanks that he has adorned you with so many titles of virtue and has made you shine forth with signs of perfection which is so great. This has brought you to the point that, having been made a diligent imitator of the Father, who is perfect, you have merited to become perfect, so that his eyes see in you nothing that is imperfect (cf Ps 138:16).

This is that perfection which will lead the King himself to seat you with him in the heavenly bridal chamber where he sits in glory upon a throne of stars. He will wish this because you have counted as of less worth the dizzy heights of a kingdom of this world and you have set down as of not so great amount the offers of an imperial marriage. You have rather been one who has sought out most holy poverty in a spirit of great humility and burning charity and in this way you have followed fast in the steps of him to whom you have merited to be joined in a true wedding.

3. Now I know very well that you are set about by many virtues and I would not want to deluge you with many words and certainly not with unneeded ones. I also know that nothing will be accounted superfluous by you if you can draw some consolation from it. But I must say this one thing, because only one thing is necessary, and I do want to admonish you by the love of him to whom you have offered yourself as a holy and pleasing sacrifice (Rom 12:1) that you be mindful of what you have set before you and that in this you be like another Rachel (Gen 29:16 ff). This will mean that you will not want to forget the point of your beginning, and that you will hold what you have, that you will do what you do, that you will not allow anything to grow slack. I wish to urge you to pass with care along the way of the beatitudes; that you be sure of step and joyful of heart and quick in response; that you walk with quick pace and light step so that you will not slip along the way nor allow your feet to become laden with dust. Have nothing to do with any who would stand in your way and would seek to turn you aside from fulfilling the vows which you have made to the Most High (Ps 49:14) and

from living in that perfection to which the Spirit of the Lord has called you.

4. Now, in order that you may walk the way of the commandments of the Lord with greater security, follow the counsel of the venerable father, our brother Elias, the Minister General. Place this ahead of the advice of others and reckon it as dearer than any other gift. If anyone tells you anything else, or if some one has something different to suggest to you which will in any way block the way to perfection for you, or which in any manner runs contrary to the vocation which you have received from God, it may well be that you should show him respect but don't do what he says. You have one aim: as a poor virgin to embrace the poor Christ *(pauperem christum virgo pauper amplectere)*. Keep your eyes fast on him who for you was reckoned of no account and let your part be to be willing to be held of no account for him. Your spouse is he who is of comeliness beyond all the sons of men (Ps 44:3), and who for your salvation became the least of men and despised and smitten and wounded in all of his body and dying under the hard requirements of the cross. It is him you want to see *(intuere)*, to gaze upon fixedly *(considerare)*, to think upon deeply *(contemplare)*, and with desire to imitate *(imitari)*.

When you suffer with him, you will reign with him; when you grieve with him, you will rejoice with him; when with him you die on the cross of harrowing demands or bitter circumstances, you will possess a heavenly dwelling place in the splendor of the saints; your name, written in the book of life, will be glorious among men. And, because you have done this, in place of the passing things of this earth, yours will be, for eternity and for ever and ever, the glory of the heavenly kingdom. In place of goods that perish yours will be the things that are eternal and you will live for ever and ever.

Farewell, dearest sister and lady also because of your union with the Lord, who is your spouse. Be sure to commend to the Lord in your devout prayers both me and my sisters who are so very happy about the good things

122

which by his grace he is bringing about in you. Remember us in every way also to your sisters.

LETTER III

1. A greeting in Christ to our sister Agnes, a lady to be held in most high regard, and one of great goodness, and worthy of love from all people of this earth. Clare, the lowliest of all and the unworthy handmaid of Christ and the servant of the Poor Ladies, sends this greeting to her who is the sister of the king of Bohemia and who is now also the sister and spouse of the most high king of heaven. To her may the author of salvation give the joys of salvation and whatever good and best thing her heart might desire.

2. I am filled with great joy because I know full well that you have gone forward with sure step and have advanced to a happy state of achievement and have won many a laurel on the course which you set for yourself to obtain the heavenly prize. I breathe with a new sense of high joy in the Lord because I know and judge as certain that, by your intent following of the footsteps of the poor and humble Christ Jesus, you make up in wondrous manner what is lacking on my part and on that of the other sisters.

In all truth I can in full measure respond in joy, nor is there any one who can take this joy from me. I have good reason for this because I possess that which I most desire to have under heaven. And I see how you have thwarted the designs of him who is the most cunning enemy and you have allowed no place for pride which devastates the human person. As I very plainly see, you have with almost terrifying thoroughness and an unexpected swiftness, as if you had just received a wondrous word of wisdom from the mouth of God, set aside the vanity which puffs up human hearts and leaves them empty. You have chosen to seek the treasure with which none other can compare (Mt 13:44). This is hidden in the field of the world and of the hearts of men. By buying it you are able to possess him by

whom all things were made out of nothing and to embrace
him in humility, in the virtue of faith and in the arms of
poverty. To use the words of the Apostle (1 Cor 3:9), by
the judgment of God himself you are the helper and one
who lifts up the languishing members of the ineffable
body of Christ.

3. Who is there then that would suggest to me that I
should not rejoice over so many causes for joy which also
prompt us to imitation? And you also, my dearest one,
want always to go forward in joy in the Lord: Do not let
bitterness wrap itself around you like a cloud, O most
dear lady of the Lord, who are the joy of the angels and
the crown of your sisters. Set your mind on the mirror of
eternity. Direct your soul to the spendor of glory. Fix
your heart on the image of the divine substance. By
contemplation transform yourself totally into the likeness
of divinity itself (Heb 1:3; 2 Cor 3:18). Then you will feel
what those who are friends feel when they taste a hidden
sweetness, which God himself from the beginning has
reserved for those who love him (Ps 30:20; 1 Cor 2:9). In
this manner you pass quickly by all those things which in
this topsy-turvy world with all its false lights hold fast
many who are ensnared in a love that is a kind of
blindness. Then you are free to love completely and
totally him who gave himself totally for love of you. The
sun and moon shine in wonder at his greatness (Divine
Office of St. Agnes). There is no limit to the abundance of
his rewards nor to their values or their greatness. He it is
who is the son of the Most High, whom a Virgin bore, and
after childbirth remained a virgin. Stay close to his most
sweet Mother who bore so great a son, whom the heavens
could not contain, and still she bore him in the narrow
cloister of her womb and as a virgin gave him birth.

Who would not shrink in horror from the snares of the
enemy of the human race, who by the proud pretense of
brief and tinsel glory strives to bring to naught what is
greater than heaven itself?

4. So dearest of all creatures, we know clearly by the
grace of God that the soul of a faithful man is greater than

124

heaven. We understand this to be true because the heavens with all other created things together can not hold the creator so that the soul of one of the faithful is alone his dwelling and his seat and this is brought about solely through love which the wicked do not possess. It is the truth who tells us this: "If any man love me, he will be loved by my Father, and I will love him, and we will come to him, and make our abode with him" (Jn 14:21). Just as the virgin of virgins who was so glorious bore him corporally in her womb, so also you who follow her footsteps can, especially by your humility and poverty, in a chaste and virginal body bear him spiritually. This you can do always and you should not have the slightest doubt about it. Then you bear within you him who bears you and all things.

You know too that one who is clothed does not dare fight with one who is naked, because he is more quickly brought to earth who offers his adversary something to grasp hold of (St. Gregory, "Homily on the Gospel," II 32-2). You understand also that no one can live in great style in this world and reign with Christ in the other life. You know it is easier for a camel to pass through the eye of a needle than for a rich man to enter heaven (Mt 19:24). You have cast aside your garments in the form of earthly riches so that you may not be wrenched down in the contest and so that you may walk along the straight way and pass through the narrow gate into the heavenly kingdom. This is a very good bit of business and worthy of praise, to leave behind the things of time in order to possess the things of eternity, to receive a hundred for one (Mt 19:29), and to possess forever the blessed life.

5. Because of all this I have thought it proper to ask your excellency and to beg of your holiness with humility, but with all the urgency I can muster, and to entreat you in the mercy of Christ to hold fast in his holy service which you have chosen. I beg you to go forward from what is good and to speed on to what is better, to press forward from virtue to virtue, so that he whom you serve with the full

yearning of your soul may deign to give you the desired reward. I ask you also in the Lord, with all the power that in me lies, that you in your holy prayers have a reward for me your servant, and a useless one, and for your other sisters here in the monastery, who have such a deep feeling for you. We ask this so that with this kind of help we may merit to enjoy the mercy of Jesus Christ and with you enjoy the eternal vision.

Farewell in the Lord and pray for me!

LETTER IV

1. To her who is the half of my soul, and who is also the sacred dwelling place of a very special love; to her who is the illustrious queen, who is the spouse of the Lamb, the Eternal King; to the lady Agnes, who is a most dear mother and sister and who is most special among all others, Clare, an unworthy servant of Christ and a useless servant of the handmaids who dwell in the Monastery of San Damiano in Assisi, sends greetings. Clare wishes for you that you be able to sing the new song before the throne of God and the Lamb and to follow the Lamb wherever he goes (Rv 14:34).

2. O mother and daughter, spouse of the King of all the ages, I have not written to you as often as I have wished to write and not nearly as many times as my soul desires and your heart too would wish. But do not think for a moment or begin to wonder that the fire of love for you in the inmost heart of your mother has been burning any less sweetly. The principal difficulty lies in the lack of messengers and in the clear presence of danger along the roads. But now, when I write in response to your love, I am lifted up in great joy with you and I wish you a full measure of happiness in the spirit, O spouse of Christ! This is my desire for you because, like that other most holy virgin, St. Agnes, you have set aside all the glittering, empty things of this world and you have been espoused in wondrous manner to the spotless Lamb who takes away

the sins of the world.

3. She is fortunate who can have part in this holy wedding, so that she with her whole heart fixes her affection upon him whose beauty all the blessed heavenly throngs admire without ceasing. His affection holds one fast; his contemplation is like a breath of new life. His kindness fills one to the brim; his sweetness is in overflowing measure. The recollection of him shines with a soft light. His fragrance revives the dead. The glorious vision of him gives beatific happiness to all the citizens of the heavenly Jerusalem. Now, since he is the splendor of eternal glory and the brightness of everlasting light and the mirror without spot (Wis 7:26), O queen, spouse of Jesus Christ, look steadfastly into this mirror every day. See in it every time you look—and look into it always—your own face. This will urge you to vest yourself totally, within and without, with adornments of all the virtues (Ps 44:10), as becomes the daughter and most chaste spouse of the highest King.

4. In this mirror you will find poverty in bright reflection. You will see there humility and love beyond words. You will be able to see this clearly with the grace of God and to contemplate it in its fullness.

Then you possess him of whom you are more sure in possession than you can be in having for your own anything else in the world. There have been kings and queens of the earth who have spun their own dreams in pride and had plans for taking over the heavens, and they walked with their heads in the clouds. But in the end it all came down as rubble and was piled up as trash.

5. Now, about these things concerning which you asked, I should respond to your loving request. You wanted to know what are the feasts which our most glorious father St. Francis instructed us to celebrate and especially about the manner of partaking of food on these days. I give it as a counsel to your prudence that first he directed us to use suitable discretion in providing for those who are weak or sick and to have for them whatever kinds of food will serve their needs. For the rest of us who are well and

strong meals for fast days are to be provided, because we fast every day, whether it is ferial or festive. Excepted from this are the Sundays and the Nativity of our Lord; on these days we are permitted to eat twice. On Thursdays, in the usual times, according to the choice of each one, no one is bound to fast. But we who are strong fast every day except Sundays and Christmas. But on every Pasch, as the writings of blessed Francis say, and on the feast of holy Mary and the holy Apostles we are not bound to fast, unless the feast days fall on Friday. But as was mentioned before, we who are healthy and strong always eat only Lenten meals.

6. However, since flesh is not cast of bronze, and since our strength is not that of a stone, and because we are fragile by nature and subject to all manner of bodily weakness, I beseech you, dearest one, to leave off any indiscreet and impossible austerity in abstinence. I beg you in the Lord that with good prudence and a large measure of discretion you withdraw from overexacting austerity into which, as I know, you had plunged yourself. I ask this so that you may be alive to praise God and so that you may render to him a reasonable service (Rom 12:1). So your sacrifice will be seasoned with the salt of prudence. May you fare well in the Lord, so indeed I greatly desire your good wishes for me. I commend myself and my sisters to your holy prayers.